The Maides Revenge by James Shirley

A TRAGEDY

As it hath been Acted with good Applause at the private house in Drury Lane, her Majesties Servants.

James Shirley was born in London in September 1596.

His education was through a collection of England's finest establishments: Merchant Taylors' School, London, St John's College, Oxford, and St Catharine's College, Cambridge, where he took his B.A. degree in approximately 1618.

He first published in 1618, a poem entitled Echo, or the Unfortunate Lovers.

As with many artists of this period full details of his life and career are not recorded. Sources say that after graduating he became "a minister of God's word in or near St Albans." A conversion to the Catholic faith enabled him to become master of St Albans School from 1623–25.

He wrote his first play, Love Tricks, or the School of Complement, which was licensed on February 10th, 1625. From the given date it would seem he wrote this whilst at St Albans but, after its production, he moved to London and to live in Gray's Inn.

For the next two decades, he would write prolifically and with great quality, across a spectrum of thirty plays; through tragedies and comedies to tragicomedies as well as several books of poetry. Unfortunately, his talents were left to wither when Parliament passed the Puritan edict in 1642, forbidding all stage plays and closing the theatres.

Most of his early plays were performed by Queen Henrietta's Men, the acting company for which Shirley was engaged as house dramatist.

Shirley's sympathies lay with the King in battles with Parliament and he received marks of special favor from the Queen.

He made a bitter attack on William Prynne, who had attacked the stage in Histriomastix, and, when in 1634 a special masque was presented at Whitehall by the gentlemen of the Inns of Court as a practical reply to Prynne, Shirley wrote the text—The Triumph of Peace.

Shirley spent the years 1636 to 1640 in Ireland, under the patronage of the Earl of Kildare. Several of his plays were produced by his friend John Ogilby in Dublin in the first ever constructed Irish theatre; The Werburgh Street Theatre. During his years in Dublin he wrote The Doubtful Heir, The Royal Master, The Constant Maid, and St. Patrick for Ireland.

In his absence from London, Queen Henrietta's Men sold off a dozen of his plays to the stationers, who naturally, enough published them. When Shirley returned to London in 1640, he finished with the Queen Henrietta's company and his final plays in London were acted by the King's Men.

On the outbreak of the English Civil War Shirley served with the Earl of Newcastle. However when the King's fortunes began to decline he returned to London. There his friend Thomas Stanley gave him help and thereafter Shirley supported himself in the main by teaching and publishing some educational works under the Commonwealth. In addition to these he published during the period of dramatic eclipse four small volumes of poems and plays, in 1646, 1653, 1655, and 1659.

It is said that he was "a drudge" for John Ogilby in his translations of Homer's Iliad and the Odyssey, and survived into the reign of Charles II, but, though some of his comedies were revived, his days as a playwright were over.

His death, at age seventy, along with that of his wife, in 1666, is described as one of fright and exposure due to the Great Fire of London which had raged through parts of London from September 2nd to the 5th.

He was buried at St Giles in the Fields, in London, on October 29th, 1666.

Index of Contents

DRAMATIS PERSONAE

Gasper De Vilarezo, an old Count, Father to Sebastiano, Catalina and Berinthia Sebastiano, sonne to Vilarezo
Antonio a lover of Berinthia, and friend to Sebastiano
Vallindras a kinsman of Antonio
Sforza, a blunt Souldier
Valasco, a lover of Berinthia
Count de Monte Nigro, a braggard
Diego, Servant to Antonio.
Signior Sharkino, a shirking Doctor
Scarabeo, a Servant to Sharkino
Daughters to Vilarezo
Catalina
Berinthia
Castabella, Sister to Antonio
Ansilva, a waiting gentle woman to the two Sisters
Nurse
Servants

To The Worthily Honoured, Henry Osborne Esquire.

Sir,

TIll I be able to give you a better proofe of my service, let not this oblation be despised. It is a Tragedy which received encouragement and grace on the English Stage; and though it come late to the Impression, it was the second birth in this kinde, which I dedicated to the Scene, as you have Art to distinguish; you have mercy and a smile, if you finde a Poem infirme through want of age, and experience the mother of strength. It is many yeares since I see these papers, which make haste to kisse your hand; if you doe not accuse the boldnesse and pride of them; I will owne the child, and beleeve Tradition so farre, that you will receive no dishonour by the acceptance; I never affected the wayes of flattery: some say I have lost my preferment, by not practising that Court sinne; but if you dare beleeve, I much honour you, nor is it upon guesse, but the taste and knowledge of your abilitie and merit; and while the Court wherein you live, is fruitfull with Testimonies of your mind, my Character is seal'd up, when I have said that your vertue hath taken up a faire lodging. Read when you have leasure, and let the Author be fortunate to be knowne

Your Servant,
JAMES SHIRLEY

THE MAIDES REVENGE

Lisbon. A Street.

Enter **SEBESTIANO, ANTONIO.**

SEBESTIANO

THe noble curtesies I have received
At Lisbone worthy friend, so much engage
That I must dye endebted to your worth,
Vnlesse you mean to accept what I've studied.
Although but partly to discharge the sums.
Due to your honour'd love.

ANTONIO

How now Sebastiano will you forfeit
The name of friend then I did hope our love
Had outgrowne complement.

SEBESTIANO

I speake my thoughts,
My tongue and heart are relatives, I thinke
I have deserved no base opinion from you;
I wish not onely to perpetuate
Our friendship, but to exchange that common name
Of friend, for

ANTONIO

What? take heede, do not prophane;
Wouldst thou be more then friend? It is a name,
Vertue can only answer to, couldst thou
Vnite into one, all goodnesse whatsoe're
Mortality can boast of, thou shalt find,
The circle narrow bounded to containe
This swelling treasure; every good admits
Degrees, but this being so good it cannot:
For he's no friend is not superlative,
Indulgent parents, brethren, kindred, tied
By the naturall flow of blood; alliances,
And what you can imagine, is to light,
To weigh with name of friend: they execute
At best, but what a nature prompts e'm to,
Are often lesse then friends, when they remaine
Our kinsmen still, but friend is never lost.

SEBESTIANO

Nay then Antonio you mistake, I meane not
To leave of friend, which with another title
Would not be lost, come them Ile tell you Sir,
I would be friend and brother, thus our friendship
Shall like a diamond set in gold not loose
His sparkling, but shew fairer; I have a paire
Of sisters, which I would commend, but that
I might seeme partiall their birth and fortunes
Deserving noble love; if thou beest free
From other faire ingagement, I would be proud
To speake them worthy, come shalt go and see them
I would not beg them sutors, fame hath spred
Through Portugall their persons, and drawne to Avero.
Many affectionate gallants.

ANTONIO

Catalina and Berinthia

SEBESTIANO

The same.

ANTONIO

Report speakes loud their beauties, and no less
Vertue in either well, I see you strive
To leave no merit where you meane to honour,
I cannot otherwise escape the censure
Of one ingratefull, but by waiting on you
Home to Avero.

SEBESTIANO

You shall honour me,
And glad my noble Father, to whom you are
No stranger, your owne worth before, hath beene
Sufficient preparation.

ANTONIO

Ha!
I have not so much choise Sebastiane,
But if one Sister of Antonios,
May have a commendation to your thoughts,
I will not spend much Art in praysing her,
Her vertue speake it selfe, I shall be happy,
And be confirmd you brother, though I misse
Acceptance at Avero.

SEBESTIANO

Still you out doe me, I could never wish
My service better plac'd, at opertunity
Ile visit you at Eluas, i'th meane time
Lets hast to Avero, where with you Ile bring
My double welcome, and not faile to second
Any designe.

ANTONIO
You shall teach me a lesson
Against we meete at Eluas Castle sit.

[Exeunt.

Avero. A Room in Vilarezo's House.

[Enter **GASPAR de VILAREZO**, and a **SERVANT**.

GASPAR DE VILAREZO
What gallants sirrab are they newly enter'd?

SERVANT
Count de Monte Nigro my Lord, and Don Valasco,

GASPAR DE VILAREZO
Give your observance then, I know their businesse;
Catalina and Berinthia are the starrs
Direct them hither, Gaspars house shall give
Respect to all, but they are two such Iewels,
I must dispose maturely, I should else
Returne ingratitude upon the heavens
For leaving me such pledges, not am I,
Like other fathers carried with the streame
Of love toth youngest, as they were in birth
They had my tendernesse, Catalina then
Is eldest in my care, Berinthia
Her childs part too, both faire and vertuous;
But daughters are held losses to a family,
Sonnes onely to maintaine honour and stemme
Alive in their posterity, and I now thinke on't,
My sonne Sebastiano hath beene slow
In his returne from Lisbone, oh that boy
Renewes my age with hope, and hath returnd
My care in education, weight for weight

With noble quality, will belov'd by the best
O' the Dons in Spaine and Portugall, whole loves
Do often threten his absence to such length
As this hath beene.

[Enter **COUNT de MONTE NIGRO** and **CATALINA**.

But here's my eldest daughter
With her amorous Count, Ile not be seene,

[Exit.

CATALINA
You have beene absent long my noble Count,
Beshrew me but I dreamt on you last night.

COUNT de MONTE NIGRO
Ha ha! did you so, I tickle her in her sleep I perceive;
Sweete Lady I did but like the valiant beast,
Give a little ground, to returne with a greater force of love.
Now by my fathers sword
And gauntlet thart a precious peece of vertue,
But priethee what didst dreame of me last night?

CATALINA
Nay 'twas an idle dreame, not worth the repitition,

COUNT de MONTE NIGRO
Thou dreamst I warrant thee, that I was fighting
For thee up to the knees in blood, why I dare doo't,
Such dreames are common with Count de monte
Nigro, my sleepes are nothing else but rehearsals of
Battels and wounds and ambuscadoes, Donzell Del Phebo
Was a mounteback of vallour, Rosicbeere a puff;
My dreames deserve to be I' the Chronicles,

CATALINA
Why, now my dreame is out,

COUNT de MONTE NIGRO
What?

CATALINA
I dreamt that you were fighting.

COUNT de MONTE NIGRO
So.

CATALINA

And that in single combate, for my sake
You slew a giant, and you no sooner had
Rescued my honour, but there crept a pigmee
Out of the earth, and kild you.

COUNT de MONTE NIGRO

Very likely, the valliantst man must dye,

CATALINA

What by a pigmee?

COUNT de MONTE NIGRO

I, thats another giant, I remember Hercules
Had a conflict with'em, oh my Dona
Catalina I well would I were so happy once to
Maintaine some honourable duell for thy sake, I shall
Nere be well, till I have kild some body; fight, tis true
I have never yet flesht my selfe in blood▪ no body
Would quarell with me, but I finde my spirit prompt
If occasion would but winke at me, why not? Wherefore has
Nature given me these brawny armes, this manly bulke,
And these Collossian supporters for nothing but to sling
The sledge, or pitch the bare, and play with
Axletrees? if thou lovest me, do but command me
Some worthy service; pox a dangers I weigh 'em no
More than fleabitings, would some body did hate that
Face, now I wish it with all my heart.

CATALINA

Would you have any body hate me?

COUNT de MONTE NIGRO

Yes, Ide hate 'em, Ide but thrust my hand into their
Mouth downe to the bottome of their bellies, plucke
Out their lungs and shake their insides outward.

[Enter **BERINTHIA** and **VALASCO**.

BERINTHIA

Noble Sir, you neede not heape more protestations,
I do beleeve you love me,

VALASCO

Doe you beleeve I love, and not accept it?

BERINTHIA

Yes I accept it too, but apprehend me

As men doe guifts, whose acceptation does not
Binde to performe what every giver craves;
Without a staine to virgin modesty
I can accept your love, but pardon me,
It is beyond my power to grant your suite.

VALASCO
Oh you too much subject a naturall guift,
And make your selfe beholding for your owne:
The Sunne hath not more right to his owne beames,
With which he gildes the day, nor the Sea lord
Of his owne waves.

BERINTHIA
Alasse, what ist to owne a passion
Without power to direct it, for I move,
Not by a motion I can call my owne,
But by a higher rapture, in obedience
To a father, and I have yet no freedome
To place affection, so you but endeere me
Without a merit.

CATALINA
Here my sister.

COUNT de MONTE NIGRO
And Don Valasco, how now, are thy arrowes feathred?

VALASCO
Well enough for roving.

COUNT de MONTE NIGRO
Roving I thought to.

VALASCO
But I hope faire.

COUNT de MONTE NIGRO
Shoot home then, Valasco I have
Presented my miseris with a paper of verses, see she
Is reading 'em.

VALASCO
Dids't make em thy selfe?

COUNT de MONTE NIGRO
My money did, what an idle question is that? as tho we
That are great men, are not furnished with stipendary

Muses. I am sure for my owne part I can buy 'em
Cheape than I can make 'em a great deale, would
You have learning have no reward?— she laughs
At them;
I am glad of that.

CATALINA
They savour of a true Poeticke fury.

COUNT de MONTE NIGRO
Do you smell nothing, something hath some savour.

CATALINA
But this line, methink hath more more feete than the rest.

COUNT de MONTE NIGRO
It should run the better for that Lady, I did it a purpose.

CATALINA
But heres another lame.

COUNT de MONTE NIGRO
That was my conceit, my owne invention, lame
Halting verses, theres the greatest Art, besides I
Thereby give you to understand, that I am valiant,
Dare cut off legs and armes at all times and make 'em
Goe halting home that are my enemies, I am
An iambographier now it is out.

CATALINA
For honours sake what's that?

COUNT de MONTE NIGRO
One of the sourest versifiers that ever crept out of
Parnassus. When I set on't. I can make any body hang himselfe
With pure Iambicks, I can fetch blood with Asclepiads;
Sting with phaleucians, whip with sapphics,
Bastinado with hexameter and pentameter, and
Yet I have a trimester left for thee my Dona Catalina.

BERINTHIA
Conclude a peace sir with your passion.
I am sory love hath beene unkind to you.
To point at me, who, till the first have knit
The sacred knot of marriage am forbid
To thinke of love.

VALASCO

But I cannot desist,
I am in love with every thing you say,
This your deniall as it comes from you
Bids me still love you, pardon faire Berinthia,
Valasco hath not power to rule himselfe;
Be you lesse faire, or vertuous, perhaps
I may abate my service.

[Enter **GASPAR de VILAREZO**, **SEBESTIANO**, and **ANTONIO**,

GASPAR de VILAREZO
Old Gaspars house is honourd by such guests,
Now by the tombe of my progenitors,
I envied, that your fame should visit me
So oft without your person, Sebestiano
Hath beene long happy in your noble friendship,
And cannot but improve himselfe in vertues,
That lives so neere your love.

CATALINA
Don Antonio de Riviero.

SEBESTIANO
The same.

CATALINA
With whose noble worth
You oft have fill'd discourse, thought your selfe happy
In his choyce friendship; if his body cary
So many graces, it is heaven within,
Where his soule is.

GASPAR de VILAREZO
Sebastiano, thou hast largely recompene'd
Thy tedious absence, you shall dishonour me,
Vnlesse you thinke your selfe as welcome here,
As at your Eluas Castle, Vilarezo
Was once as you are sprightly, and though I say it
Maintained my fathers reputation,
And honour of our house with actions
Worthy our name and family, but now,
Time hath let fall cold snow upon my haires,
Ploughed on my browes the furrowes of his anger
Disfurnishd me of active blood, and wrapt me
Halfe in my seare cloth, yet I have minde
That bids me honour vertue, where I see it
Bud forth and spring so hopefully,

ANTONIO
You speake all noblenesse, and encourage me
To spend the greenness of my rising yeares
So to th' advantage, that at last I may
Be old like you.

GASPAR de VILAREZO
Daughters speake his welcome, Catalina!

CATALINA
Sir, you are most welcome.

COUNT de MONTE NIGRO
How's that? she sayes he is most welcome, he were
Not best love her, she never made me such a reverence
For all the kisses I have bestowed upon her since
I first opened my affection, I do not like this
Follow, I must be faire to use doctor Sharkins cunning,

VALASCO
It were not truely noble to affront him;
My blood boyles in me, it shall I coole againe,
The place is venerable by her presence,
And I may be deceiv'd, Valasco then
Keepe distance with thy feares.

ANTONIO
How now Antonio, where hast thou loft thy selfe?
Strucke dead with Ladies eyes? I could star-gaze
For ever thus, oh pardon love, gainst whom
I often have prophan'd, and mockd thy fires,
Thy flames now punish me, let me collect:
They are both excellent creatures, there is
A Majestie in Catalina's eye, and every part carries ambition
Or Queene upon it, yet Berinthia's
Hath something more than all this praise, though she
Command the world, this hath more power o'er me
Here I have lost my freedome, not the Queene
Of love could thus have wounded poore Antonio'
I'll speake to her; Lady I'm an Novice, yet in love.

BERINTHIA
It may be so.

ANTONIO [aside]
She jests at me, yet I should be proud to be
Your servant.

BERINTHIA
I entertaine no servants that are proud.

VALASCO
Divine Berinthia!

ANTONIO
She checks my rudenesse that so openly
I seem to court her, and in presence too
Of some that have engaged themselves perhaps,
To her already.

GASPAR de VILAREZO
Come let us in, my house spreads to receive you,
Which you may call your owne, Ile leade the way.

CATALINA
Please you walke Sir.

ANTONIO
It will become me thus to waite on you.

[Exeunt all but **COUNT de MONTE NIGRO** and **VALASCO**.

COUNT de MONTE NIGRO
Does not the foole ride us both?

VALASCO
What foole? both, whom?

COUNT de MONTE NIGRO
That foole, both us, we are but horses and may
Walke one another for ought I see before the doore, when he
Is alight and entred, I do not relish that same
Novice, he were not best gull me; harke you Don
Valasco, what shals doe?

VALASCO
Doe, why?

COUNT de MONTE NIGRO
This Antonio is a sutor to one of 'em.

VALASCO
I feare him not.

COUNT de MONTE NIGRO
I do not feare him neither, I dare fight with him, and

He were ten Antonios, but the Ladies, don, the Ladies.

VALASCO
Berinthia, to whom
I pay my love devotions, in my eare
Seemd not to welcome him, your Lady did.

COUNT de MONTE NIGRO
I but for all that he had most mind to your mistris,
And I do not see but if he pursue it,
There is a possibility to scale the fort, Ladies
Mindes may alter, by your favour, I have lesse
Cause to feare o'th two; if ht love not Catalina
My game is free, and I may have a course in
Her Parke the more easily.

VALASCO
Tis true, he preferred service to Berinthia,
And what is she then to resist the vowes
Antonio if he love, dare heape upon her?
He's gracious with her father, and a friend
Deere as his bosome to Sebastiano,
And may be is directed by that brother
To aime at her, or if he make free choyce,
Berinthias beauty will draw up his soule.

COUNT de MONTE NIGRO
And yet now I thinke on't, he was very sawey
With my love to support her arme, which she
Accepted too familiarly, and she should
But love him, it were as bad for me, for tho he care
Not for her, I am sure she will never abide me after it,
By this hilts I must kill him, theres no remedy,
I cannot helpe it.

VALASCO
Ile know my destiny.

[Exit.

COUNT de MONTE NIGRO
And I my fate but here he comes.

[Enter **ANTONIO**.

ANTONIO
The strangest resolution of a father
I ever heard, I was covetous

To acquaint him with my wishes, praid his leave
I might be servant to Berinthia,
But thus he briefly answered, untill
His eldest daughter were dispos'd in marriage
His youngest must not love, and therefore wisht me
Unlesse I could place Catalina here,
Leave off soliciting, yet I was welcome,
You fed on nothing but Berinthia,
From whose faire eyes love threw a thousand flames
Unto Antonio's heart, her cheeks bewraying
As many amorous blushings, which brake out
Like a forc'd lightning from a troubled cloud,
Discovering a restraint, as if within
She were at conflict, which her colour onely
Tooke liberty to speake, but soone fell backe,
And as it were checkt by silence.

COUNT de MONTE NIGRO
Ile stay no longer, sir a word with you, are you desperat?

ANTONIO
Desperate, why sit?

COUNT de MONTE NIGRO
I aske and you be desperate, are you weary of your
Life, and you be, say but the word; some body can tell
How to dispatch you without a physitian, at a minuits warning.

ANTONIO
You are thē noble Count de monte Nigro.

COUNT de MONTE NIGRO
I care not a Spanish fig what you count me, I must
Call you to account sir; in briefe the Lady
Dona Catalina is my mistris, I do not meane to be bass •ed
While this toole has any steele in't, and I have some
Mettall in my selfe too.

ANTONIO
The Dona Catalina? do you love her?

[Enter **GASPAR de VILAREZO**, **CATALINA** and **BERINTHIA**.

BERINTHIA
She is a Lady in whom onely lives
Natures and Arts perfection, borne to shame
All former beauties, and to be the wonder

Of all succeeding, which shall fade and wither
When she is but remembred.

COUNT de MONTE NIGRO
I can endure no more, Diablo, he is mortally in love
With Catalina.

GASPAR de VILAREZO
Tis so, he's tane with Catalinaes beautie.

COUNT de MONTE NIGRO
Sir I am a servant of that Lady, therefore eate up
Your words, or you shall be sensible that I am Count
De Monte Nigro, and she's no dish for Don Antonio.

ANTONIO
Sir I will do you right.

COUNT de MONTE NIGRO
Or I will right my selfe.

CATALINA
He did direct those prayses unto me
This doth confirme it.

BERINTHIA
He cannot so soone alter,
I shall discover a passion through my eyē.

COUNT de MONTE NIGRO
Thou shewest thy selfe a noble Gentleman, the
Count is now thy friend.

ANTONIO
Does it become me sir, to prosecute
Where such a noble Count is interessed,
Vpon my soule I wish the Lady yours,
Here my suite fals, with tender of my servicē;
Would you were married, nay in bed together
My honourable Count.

CATALINA
Your face is cloudy sir, as you suspected
Your presence were not welcome; had you naught
But title of a brothers friendship, it were
Enough to oblige us to you, but your worth
In Catalinaes eies, bids me proclaime you

A double acceptation.

ANTONIO
Oh, you are bounteous Ladie.

COUNT de MONTE NIGRO
Sir—

ANTONIO
Doe not feare me,
I am not worthie your opinion,
It shall be happinesse for me to kisse
This Ivory hand,

COUNT de MONTE NIGRO
The whilst I kisse her lip and be immotall.

SEBESTIANO
Antonio my father is a rocke,
In that he first resolved, and I account it part of my
Owne unhappinesse, I hope you hold me not suspected,

ANTONIO
I were unworthy such a friend, his care
Becomes him nobly; has not younder Count
Some hope of Catalina.

SEBESTIANO
My father thinkes that sister worthy of
More than a bare Nobility.

ANTONIO
Ile backe to Elvas noble sir,
This entertainement is so much above
Antonio's merit, if I leave you not
I shall be out of hope to —

GASPAR de VILAREZO
Nay then you mocke me sir, you must not leave me
Without discourtesie so soone, we trissle time,
This night you are my guest, my honored Count,
My Don Valasco.

COUNT de MONTE NIGRO
Yes my Lord, wee'le follow.

ANTONIO
Ha I am resolv'd, like Barge-men when they row.
Ile looke auother way then that I goe.

[Exeunt.

The Same. A Room in Vilarezo's House.

Enter **CATALINA** and **ANSILVA**.

CATALINA
Ansilva yon observe with curious eye
All Gentlemen that come hither, whats your opinion.
Of Don Antonio?

ANSILVA
My opinion Madam, I want Art.
To judge of him.

CATALINA
Then without Art your judgement.

ANSILVA
He is one of the most accomplisht Gentlemen
Ansilva ere beheld, pardon Madam.

CATALINA
Nay, it doth not displease, 'yare not alone,
He hath friends to second you, and who dost thinke
Is cause he tarrries here.

ANSILVA
Your noble father will not let him goe.

CATALINA
And canst thou see no higher? then thou art dull.

ANSILVA
Madam, I guesse at something more.

CATALINA
What?

ANSILVA
Love?

CATALINA
Of whom?

ANSILVA
I know not that.

CATALINA
How not that? Thou'dst bring thy former truth
Into suspition, why tis more apparant
Then that he loves.

ANSILVA
If judging eyes may guide him,
I know where he should' chuse, but I have heard
That love is blind.

CATALINA
Ha!

ANSILVA
Vertue would direct him Madam unto you, I know not his
Obedience, I shall repent if I offend.

CATALINA
Tha'rt honest, be yet more free, hide not a thought that may concerne it.

ANSILVA
Then Madam I thinke he loves my Lady Berinthia;
I have observ'd his eyes rowle that way,
Even now I spied him
Close with her in the Arbour, pardon me Madam.

CATALINA
Th'ast done me faithfull service, be yet more vigilant,
I know thou speakst all truth, I doe suspect him,

[Exit **ANSILVA**.

My sister, ha! Dare shee maintaine contention?
Is this the dutie bindes her to obey
A fathers precepts, tis dishonour to me.

[Enter **ANSILVA**.

ANSILVA
Madam, heres a pretty hansome stripling new alight,
Enquires for Don Antonio.

CATALINA
Let me see him, 'twill give me good occasion to be
My owne observer;

[Enter **DIEGO**.

Whom would you sir?

DIEGO
I am sent in quest of Antonio.

CATALINA
He speakes like a Knight errant, he comes in quest,

DIEGO
I have heard it a little vertue in some Spanniels to
Quest now and then Lady.

CATALINA
But you are none.

DIEGO
My Mr. cannot beate me from him Madam, I am one of
The oldest appurtenances belonging to him, and yet I
Have little mosse in my chinne.

CATALINA
The more to come, a wittie knave.

DIEGO
No more wit then will keep my head warme, I beseech you amiable Virgin help my Master Antonio to
some intelligence that a servant of his waits to speake with him from his sister Madona Castabella.

CATALINA
It shall not neede sir, Ile give him notice my selfe,
Ansilva Entertaine time with him.

[Exit.

ANSILVA
A promising young man [aside].

DIEGO
Doe you waite on this Lady?

ANSILVA
Yes sir.

DIEGO
Wee are both of a tribe then, though wēe differ in our sexe, I beseech you taxe me not of immodesty, or want of breeding, that I did not salute you upon the first view of your person, this kisse be as good as presse-mony to bind me to your service.

[Kisses her.

ANSILVA
'Yare very welcome, by my virginity.

[Exit.

DIEGO
Your virginitie a good word to save an oath, for all she made me a curtesy, it was not good manners to leave mee so soone 'yare very welcome by my virginity; was she afraid of breaking, it may be she is crack'd already, but here she is againe.

[Enter **ANSILVA**.

ANSILVA
May I begge your name sir?

DIEGO
No begger sweet, would you have it at length, then
My name is Signior Baltazaro Clere Mautado,
But for brevities sake they call me Diego.

ANSILVA,
Then Signior Diego once more you are welcome.

DIEGO
Bazelez manes Signiora, and what my tongue is not able to expresse, my head shall; it seemes you have liv'd long a Virgin.

ANSILVA
Not above seven or eight and thirty yeares.

DIEGO
By Lady a tried Virgin, you have given the world
A large testimony of your virginity.

[Exeunt.

The Same. A Garden.

[Enter **ANTONIO, BERINTHIA. CATALINA** following at a distance.

BERINTHIA
I should be thus a disobedient daughter
A Fathers Hests are sacred.

ANTONIO
But in love
They have no power, it is but tyranny,
Plaine usurpation to command the minde
Against its owne election; I am yours,
Vow'd yours for ever, send me not away
Shipwrack'd ith' habour, say but you can love me,
And I will waite an age, not wish to move
But by commission from you, to whom
I render the possession of my selfe—

[Discovers **CATALINA**.

Ha! we are betrai'd, I must use cunning,
She lives in you, and take not in worse sence;
You are more gracious, in that you are
So like your eldest sister, in whom lives
The coppy of so much perfection,
All other seemē to imitate.

CATALINA
Does he not praise me now?

[Comes forward.

ANTONIO
But here she is,
Madam, not finding you ith' garden,
I met this Lady.

CATALINA
I came to tell you
A servant of yours attends with letters from
Your sister Madona Castabella.

[Enter **DIEGO**.

ANTONIO
Diego what newes?

DIEGO
Sir, my Lady remembers her love, these letters informe you the state of all things.

[**ANTONIO** walks aside with the letters.

CATALINA
What serious conference had you sister with that Gentleman.

BERINTHIA
Would you had heard them sister, they concern'd your Commendations.

CATALINA
Why should he not deliver them to my selfe.

BERINTHIA
It may be then
You would have thought he flattered.

CATALINA
I like not this rebound,
Tis fairest to catch at fall.

BERINTHIA
Sister, I hope
You have no suspition, I have courted
His stay or language on my life no accent
Fell from me, your owne eare would not have heard
With acceptation.

CATALINA
It may be so, and yet I dare acquit you,
In duty to a Father, you would wish me
All due respect, I know it.

ANTONIO
Diego.

DIEGO
Sir.

ANTONIO
You observe the waiting creatures in the blacke,

Harke [Whispers to him] you apprehend me.

DIEGO
With as much tenacity as a servant.

CATALINA
I hope sir, now we shall enjoy you longer.

ANTONIO
The gods would sonner be sicke with Nectar, than Antonio
Crow weary of such faire societie;
But I am at home expected, a poore sister,
My fathers care alive, and dying was
His Legacy, having out-staid my time
Is tender of my absence.

[Enter **GASPAR de VILAREZO, SEBASTIANO, COUNT de MONTE NIGRO** and **VALASCO**.

CATALINA
My Lord Antonio meanes to take his leave.

GASPAR de VILAREZO
Although last night you were inclin'd to goe,
Let us prevaile this morning.

CATALINA
A servant of his, he saies, brought letters
To hasten departure.

GASPAR de VILAREZO
Why sirra, will you rob us of your master.

DIEGO
Not guilty my Lord.

COUNT de MONTE NIGRO
Sir, if you'le needs go, we'le bring you on your way.

ANTONIO
I humbly thank your honour, Ile not be so trouble some.

COUNT de MONTE NIGRO
Would you were gone once, I doe not meane to trouble my selfe so much I warrant thee [aside].

ANTONIO
I have now a charge upon me, I hope it may
Excuse me, if I hasten my returne.

GASPAR de VILAREZO

Tis faire, and reasonable, well sir, my sonne
Shall waite on you oth' way, if any occasion
Draw you to Avero, lets hope you'le see us,
You know your welcome.

ANTONIO

My Lord the favours done me, would proclaime
I were too much unworthy not to visit you,
Oft as I see Avero; Madam I part with some unhappinesse
To lose your presence, give me leave I may
Be absent your admirer, to whose memory
I write my selfe a servant,

COUNT de MONTE NIGRO

Poxe on your complemênt, you were not best write
In her table-bookes.

CATALINA

You doe not know
What power you have o're me, that but to please you
Can frame my selfe to take a leave so soone.

VALASCO

What thinke you of that my Lord?

COUNT de MONTE NIGRO

Why, she sayes she has power to take her leave
So soone, no hurt ath' world in't, I hope she is an
Innocent Lady [To **BERINTHIA**].

ANTONIO

The shallow rivers glide away with noise,
The deepe are silent, fare you well Lady.

COUNT de MONTE NIGRO

I told you he is a shallow fellow.

VALASCO

I know not what to thinke on't Berinthia.

ANTONIO

Gentlemen happinesse and successe in your desires.

SEBESTIANO

Ile see you a league or two.

GASPAR de VILAREZO
By any meanes, nay sir.

ANTONIO
Diego.

DIEGO
My Lord I have a suite to you before I goe.

GASPAR de VILAREZO
To me Diego, prethee speake it.

DIEGO
That while other Gentlemen are happy to devide their affections among the Ladies, I may have your honours leave to beare some good-will to this Virgin: Cupid hath throwne a dart at me, like a blinde buzzard as he was, and theres no recovery without a cooler; if I be sent into these parts, I desire humbly I may be bold to rub acquaintance with Mistresse Ansilva.

GASPAR de VILAREZO
With all my heart Diego.

DIEGO
Madam, I hope you will not be an enemy to a poore
Flye that is taken in the flame of the blind god.

CATALINA
You shall have my consent sir.

GASPAR de VILAREZO
But what say a Ansilva, hast thou a mind to a husband?

ANSILVA
I feare I am too young seven yeares hence were time enough for me.

SEBESTIANO
Shees not full fortie yet sir.

DIEGO
I honour the Antiquitie of her maidenhead, thou
Mistresse of my heart.

ANTONIO
Come lets away Diego our horses—

GASPAR de VILAREZO
We'le bring you to the gate.

COUNT de MONTE NIGRO
Yes, wee'le bring him out of doores, would wee were shut of him.

[Exeunt all but **ANSILVA**.

ANSILVA
Hay ho, who would have thought I should have benne in love with a stripling, have I seene so many maiden-heades snffer before me, and must mine come to the blocke at fortie yeares old, if this Diego have the grace to come on, I shall have no power to keepe my selfe chast any longer; how many maides have beene overrunne with this love? but heres my Lady.

[Exit.

SCENE III

the Same.

[Enter **CATALINA** and **VALASCO**.

CATALINA
Sir, you love my sister.

VALASCO
With an obedient heart.

CATALINA
Where do you think Don Antonio hath made choice
To place his love?

VALASCO
There where I wish it may grow older in desire,
And be crown'd with fruitfull happinesse.

CATALINA
Hath your affection had no deeper roote,
That tis rent up already, I had thought
It would have stood a Winter, but J see
A Summer storme hath kil'd it, fare you well sir.

[Going.

VALASCO
How's this, a Summers storme!
Lady by the honour of your birth,
Put off these cloudes, you maze me, take off

The wonder you have put upon Valasco,
And solve these riddles.

CATALINA
You love Berinthia.

VALASCO
With a devoted heart, else may I die
Contempt of all mankinde, not my owne soule
Is deerer to me.

CATALINA
And yet you wish Antonio may be crown'd
With happinesse in his love, he loves Birinthia.

VALASCO
How?

CATALINA
Beyond expression, to see how a good nature
Free from dishonour in it selfe, is backward
To thinke another guilty, suffers it selfe
Be poisoned with opinion, did your eyes
Emptie their beames so much in admiration
Of your Berinthias beauty, you left none
To observe your owne abuses,

VALASCO
Doth not Antonio dedicare his thoughts
To your acceptance, 'tis impossible,
I heard him praise you to the heavens, above 'em;
Made himselfe hoarse but to repeate your vertues
As he had beene in extasie; love Birinthia?
Hell is not blacker than his soule, if he
Love any goodnesse but your selfe.

CATALINA
That lesson he with impudence hath reade
To my owne eares, but shall I tell you sir?
We are both made but properties to raise
Him to his partiall ends, flattery is
The stalkeing horse of pollicy, saw you not,
How many flames he shot into her eyes
When they were parting, for which she pay'd backe
Her subtill teares, he wrung her by the hand,
Seem'd with the greatnesse of his passion
To have beene o're borne, Oh cunning treachery!
Worthy our justice, true be commended me;

But could you see the Fountaine that sent forth
So many cozening streames, you would say Styx
Were Christ all to it, and wast not to the Count,
Whom he suppos'd was in pursuite of me;
Nay, whom he knew did love me, that he might
Fire him she more to consummate my marriage
That I disposed he might have of accesse
To his belov'd Berinthia, the end
Of his desires I can confirme it, he praid
To be so happy with my fathers leave
To be her amorous servant, which he nobly
Denied, partly expressing your engagements;
If you have least suspition of this truth:
But dee' thinke she love you?

VALASCO
I cannot challenge her, but she has let fall
Something to make me hope, how thinke you shee's
Affected to Antonio?

CATALINA
May be
Luke warme as yet, but soone as as shees caught,
Inevitably his, without prevention.
For my owne part I hate him in whom lives
A will to wrong a Gentleman, for hee was
Acquainted with your love, 'twas my respect
To tender so your injury, I could not
Be silent in it. What you meane to doe
I leave to your owne thoughts.

[Going.

VALASCO
Oh stay sweete Lady, leave me not to struggle
Alone with this universall affliction;
You speake even now Berinthia would be his
Without prevention, oh that Antidote,
That Balsome to my wound.

CATALINA
Alas I pitty you, and the more, because
I see your troubies so amaze your judgement,
Ile tell you my opinion sir oth' sudden;
For him, he is not worth Valasco's anger;
Onely thus, you shall discover to my Father,
She promis'd you her love, be confident
To say you did exchange faith to her; this alone

May chance assure her, and if not I hav't:
Steale her away, your love I see is honourable,
So much I suffer when de sert is wounded,
You shall have my assistance, you apprehend me,

VALASCO
I am devoted yours, command me ever.

CATALINA
Keepe smooth your face, and still maintaine your worship
With Berinthia, things must be manag'd
And strucke in the maturity, noble sir; I wish
You onely fortunate in Berinthias love.

VALASCO
Words are too poore to thanke you, I looke on you
As my safe guiding starre.

[Exit.

CATALINA
But I shall prove a wandering starre, I have
A course which I must finish for my selfe.
Glide on thou subtill mover, thou hast brought
This instrument already for thy aymes,
Sister, Ile breake a Serpents egge betimes,
And teare Antonio from thy very bosome,
Love is above all law of nature, blood,
Not what men call, but what that bides is good.

[Exit.

SCENE IV

Elvas. A Room in the Castle.

[Enter **CASTABELLA** and **VILLANDRAS**.

GASPAR DE VILAREZO
Be not so carefull Cooze, your brothers well.
Be confident if he were otherwise
You should have notice, whom hath he to share
Fortunes without you? all his ills are made
Lesse by your bearing part, his good is doubled
By your communichaing.

CASTABELLA

By this reason
All is not well, in that my ignorance
What fate hath hapned, barres me off the portion
Belongs to me sister, but my care
Is so much greater, in that Diego whom
I charg'd to put on wings, if all were well,
Is dull in his returne.

[Enter **ANTONIO** and **DIEGO**.

GASPAR DE VILAREZO

His Master happily hath commanded him
To attend him homewards, this is recompenc'd
Already, looke they are come;
Y'are welcome sir.

ANTONIO

Oh sister, ere you let fall words of welcome,
Let me unlade a treasure in your eare
Able to weigh downe man.

CASTABELLA

What treasure brother, you amaze me,

ANTONIO

Never was man so blest,
As heavens had studied to enrich me here,
So am I fortunate.

GASPAR DE VILAREZO

You make me covetous.

ANTONIO

I have a friend.

GASPAR DE VILAREZO

You have a thousand sir, is this your treasure?

ANTONIO

But I have one more worth then millions,
And he doth onely keepe alive that name
Of friendship in his breast, pardon Villandros,
Tis not to straine your love, whom I have tried,
My worthiest cozen.

CASTABELLA

But where is this same friend, why came he not
To Eluas with you, sure he cannot be
Deare to you Brother, to whom I am not indebted
At least for you.

DIEGO

I have many deare friends too, my Taylor is one
To whom I am indebted

ANTONIO

His Commission
Stretch'd not so farre, a Fathers tie was on him,
But I have his noble promise, er't be long,
We shall enjoy him.

CASTABELLA

Brother I hope
You know how willingly I can entertaine
Your blisse, and make it mine, pray speake the man
To whom we owe so much.

ANTONIO

Twere not charity to starve you thus with shaddowes,
Take him and with him in thy bosome locke
The Mirrour of fidelity, Don Sebastiano.

CASTABELLA

I oft have heard you name him full of worth,
And upon that relation have laid up,
One deare to my remembrance.

ANTONIO

But he must be dearer Castabella, harke you sister,
I have beene bold upon thy vertue, to
Invite him to you, if your heart be free.
Let it be empty ever, if he doe not
Fill it with noblest love, to make relation,
What zeale he gave of a worthy nature,
At our last parting (when betwixt a sonne,
And friend he so divided his affections
And out did both) you would admire him: were
I able I would build a temple where
We tooke our leave,
The ground it selfe was hallowed
So much with his owne piety, Diego saw it.

DIEGO

Yes sir, I saw, heard, and wondred.

ANTONIO

Come I will tell you all, to your chamber sister,
Diego, our plot must on, all time is lost
Vntill we try the mooving.

DIEGO

If the plot please you sir, let me alone to play my part
I warrant you.

ANTONIO

Come Castabella, and prepare to heare
A story not of length but worthy your eare.

[Exeunt

SCENE V

Avero. A Room in Vilarezo's House.

[Enter **GASPAR de VILAREZO**, **VALASCO** and **CATALINA**.

GASPAR DE VILAREZO

You have not dealt so honourably sir,
As did become you, to proceed so far
Without my knowledge, give me leave to tell you
You are not welcome.

VALASCO

My Lord I am sorry,
If I have any way trangrest, I was not
Respectlesse of your honour, nor my fame,
Valasco shall be unhappy, if by him
You shall derive a staine, my actions faire,
I have done nothing with Berinthia,
To merit such a language, twas not ripe,
For me to interrupt the father, when I knew not
What grace I hold with her.

GASPAR de VILAREZO

Hell on her grace, is this her duty? ha,
I can forget my nature if she dare
Make so soone for feit of her piety;

Oh where is that same awfull dread of Parent,
Should live in children; tis her ambition
To out runne her sister, but Ile curbe her impudence,

CATALINA
Retire your selfe, this passion must have way,
This workes as I would have it, feare nothing sir,
Obscure.

[Exit **VALASCO**.

GASPAR DE VILAREZO
Ile cloyster her, and starve this spirit
Makes her deceive my trust; Catalina
Vpon thy duty I command thee, take
Her custody on thee, keepe her from the eye
Of all that come to Averro, let her discourse
With pictures on the wall, I feare she hath
Forgot to say her prayers, is she growne sensuall?

CATALINA
But my Lord.

GASPAR DE VILAREZO
Oh keepe thy accents for a better cause,
She hath contemd us both, thou caust not see
What blemish she derives unto our name.
Yet these are sparkes, he hath a fire within,
Will turne all into flames, wheres Valasco?

CATALINA
Good sir, a much afflicted worthy Gentleman,
At your displeasure.

GASPAR DE VILAREZO
Thou art too full of pitty, nay th'art cruell
To thy owne fame, he must not have accesse
To prosecute, it was my doting sinne,
Of too much confidence in Berinthia,
Gave her such libertie, on my blessing punish it,
Twill be a vertuous act, the snow I thought
Was not more innocent, more cold, more chaste
Why my command bound her in ribs of ice,
But shees dissolv'd, to thee Ile leave her now,
Be the maintainer of thy Fathers vow,

[Exit

VALASCO
Why I am undone now,

CATALINA
Nothing lesse, this conflict
Prepares your peace, I am her guardian,
Love smiles upon you, I am not inconstant,
Having more power to assist you, but away,
We must not be discri'd, expect ere long
To heere what you desire.

VALASCO
My blisse I remember.

[Exit

CATALINA
Berinthia, y'are my prisoner, at my leisure
Ile studdy on your fate, I cannot be
Friend to my selfe, when I am kind to thee.

[Exit

ACTUS III

SCENE I

The Same. A Gallery in Vilarezo's House.

Enter **SEBASTIANO, BERINTHIA, ANSILVIA, DIEGO** meetes them.

SEBESTIANO
Welcome honest Diego, your Master Antonio is in health I hope.

DIEGO
He commanded me, remember his service to you, I have obtaind his leave for a small absence to perfect a suite I lately commenc'd in this Court.

SEBESTIANO
You follow it close me thinks Berinthia, I see this cloud
Vanish already, be not dejected, soone
Ile know the depth on't. Should the world forsake thee,
Thou shalt not want a brother deere Berinthia.

[Exit

[Secretly gives **BERINTHIA** a Letter.

DIEGO
This is my Lady Berinthia, prethee let me shew
Some manners, Madam my Master Antonio speakes his
Service to you in this paper: alas Madam, I was but
Halfe at home, and I am returnd to see if I can recover
The tother peece of my selfe, so, was it not a reasonable
Complement [To **ANSILVA**].

BERINTHIA
Antonio, he's constant I perceive.

[Exit

DIEGO
So, we are alone, sweet Mistresse Ansilva, J am bold
To renue my suite, which least it should either
Fall or depend too long having past my declaration,
I shall desire to come to a judgement.
My cause craves noching but justice,
That is, that you would be mine; and now since
You selfe is judge also, I beseech you be not partiall
In your owne cause, but give seatence for the plaintiffe, and
I will discharge the fees of the Court on this fashion.

[Kisses her.

[Enter **BERINTHIA**.

BERINTHIA
Here is a haven yet to rest my soule on,
In midst of all unhappinesse, which I looke on,
With the same comfort a distressed Sea man
Afar off, viewes the coast he would enjoy,
When yet the Seas doe tosse his reeling barke,
Twixt hope and danger, thou shalt be conceald.

[She mistaking as she moved put up the Letter, it falls to the ground.

ANSILVA
Here's my Lady Berinthia.

DIEGO
What care I for my Lady Berinthia, and she thinkes
Much, would she had one to stopp her mouth.

ANSILVA
But I must observe her, upon her fathers displeasure,
She is committed to my Ladies custody, who hath made
Me her keeper, she must be lockt up.

DIEGO
Ha lockt up.

ANSILVA
Madam, it is now time you would retire to your owne Chamber.

BERINTHIA
Yes, prethee doe Ansilva in this gallery,
I breathe but too much aire, oh Diego youle have
An answer I perceive, ere you returne.

[Exeunt **BERINTHIA** and **ANSILVA**.

DIEGO
My journey were to no purpose else, Madam—I apprehend her; ile waite an opportunity, alas poore lady, is my sweete heart become a jaylor, there's hope of an office without money.

[Enter **ANSILVA** hastily.

ANSILVA
Diego! I spy my Lady Catalina comming this way, pray shrowd your selfe behinde this cloth, I would be loath shee should ice us here together, quickely, I heare her treading,

[**DIEGO** retires behind the hangings.

CATALINA [within]
Ansilva.

ANSILVA
Madam.

CATALINA [within]
Who's with you?

ANSILVA
No body Madam.

[Enter **CATALINA**.

CATALINA
Was not Diego with you, Antonioes man?

ANSILVA
He went from me Madam halfe an houre agoe,
To visit friends ith' City.

CATALINA
He hath not seene Berinthia I hope.

ANSILVA
Unlesse he can pierce stone walls Madam, I am sure.

CATALINA
Direct Don Valasco hither by the backe staires,
I expect him.

ANSILVA
I shall Madam.

CATALINA
Ha! whats this? a Letter to Berinthia! from whom?
Subscrib'd? Antonio! what devill brought this hither?
Furies torment me not, [Reads] While I am Antonio, expect
Not I can be other then thy servant, all my thoughts
Are made sacred with thy remembrance, whose hope
Sustaines my life, oh I drink poyson from these fatall accents,
Be thy soule blacker then the inke that staines
The cursed paper, would each droppe had falne
From both your hearts, and every Character
Been tex'd with blood, I would have tir'd mine eyes
To have read you both dead here, upon my life
Diego hath beene the cunning Mercury
In this conveyance, J suspect his love
Is but a property to advance this suite.
But I will crosse them all;

[Enter **VALASCO**.

Don Valasco, you are seasonably arriv'd,
I have a Letter for you.

VALASCO
For me?

CATALINA
It does concerne you.

[Gives him the letter, which he reads.

VALASCO

Ha!

CATALINA
How doe you like it sir?

VALASCO
As I should a Punyard sticking here, how came
You by it?

CATALINA
I found it here by accident oth'ground,
I am sure it did not grow there, I suppose
Diego, the servant of Antonio
Who colourably pretends affection
To Ansilva, brought it, hees the agent for him.
Now the designe appeares, day is not more conspicuous
Then this cunning.

VALASCO
I am resolv'd,

CATALINA
For what?

VALASCO
Antonio or I must change our ayre,
This is beyond my patience▪ sleepe in this
And never wake to honour, oh my fates,
He takes the freehold of my soule away,
Berinthia, and it, are but one creature,
I have beene a tame foole all this while,
Swallowed my poyson in a fruitelesse hope,
But my revenge, as heavy as loves wrath,
Wrapt in a thunderbolt is falling on him,

CATALINA
Now you appeare all noblenesse, but collect
Draw up your passions to a narrow point
Of vengeance, like a burning glasse that fires
Surest ith smallest beame, he that would kill,
Spends not his idle fury to make wounds,
Farre from the heart of him he fights withall,
Looke where you most can danger, let his head
Bleed out his braines, or eyes, aime at that part
Is deerest to him, this once put to hazzard,
The rest will bleed to death.

VALASCO

Apply this Madam.

CATALINA
The time invites to action, ile be briefe,
Strike him through Berinthia.

VALASCO
Ha!

CATALINA
Mistake me not, I am her sister,
Shee is his heart, make her your owne, you have
A double victory, thus you may kill him
With most revenge, and give your owne desires,
A most confirm'd possession, fighting with him,
Can be no conquest to you, if you meane
To strike him dead, pursue Berinthia,
And kill him with the wounds he made at you,
It will appeare but justice, all this is
Within your fathom sir.

VALASCO
Tis some divinity hangs on your tongue.

CATALINA
If you consent Berinthia shall not see,
More sunnes till you enjoy her.

VALASCO
How deere Madam.

CATALINA
Thus you shall steale her away

VALASCO
Oh, when?

CATALINA
Provide
Such trusty friends, but let it not be knowne
Upon your honour, I assist you in't.
And after midnight when soft sleep hath charm'd
All sesces, enter at the Garden gate,
Which shall to open for you, to know her chamber,
A candle shall direct you in the Window,
Ansilva shall attend too, and provide
To give you entrance, thence take Berinthia,
And soone convey her to what place you think

Secure and most convenient, in small time
You may procure your owne conditions.
But sir you must engage your selfe to use her
With honourable respects, she is my sister,
Did not I thinke you noble, for the world
I would not runne that hazzard.

VALASCO
Let heaven forsake me then, was ever mortall
So bound to womans care, my mothers was
Halfe paid her at my birth, but you have made me
An everlasting debtor.

CATALINA
Select your friend, bethinke you of a place
You may transpose her.

VALASCO
I am all wings.

[Exit.

CATALINA
So, when gentle physicke will not serve, we must
Apply more active, but there is
Yet a receipt behind; Valasco's shallow,
And will be planet strucke, to see Berinthia
Dye in his armes: tis so, yet he himselfe
Shall carry the suspition, if art,
Or hell can furnish me with such a poyson,
Sleepe thy last sister, whilst thou livest I have,
No quiet in my selfe, my rest thy grave.

[Exit

[**DIEGO** comes from behinde the hangings.
Goe thy wayes, and the devill wants a brerder thou
Art for him, one spirit and her selfe are able to furnish
Hell and it were unprovided; but I am glad I heard all
I shall love hangings the better while I live:
I pereive some good may be done behind them
But ile acquaint my Lady Berinthia,
Heres her chamber I observ'd: Madam!
Madam Berinthia!

[**BERINTHIA** appears above.

BERINTHIA

Whose there?

DIEGO
Tis I Diego, I am Diego.

BERINTHIA
Honest Diego, what good newes,

DIEGO
You're undone, undone lost, undone for ever; it is time now to be serious.

BERINTHIA
Ha,

DIEGO
Wheres my Master Antonioes Letter.

BERINTHIA
Here, where, ha, alas, I feare I have lost it.

DIEGO
Alas you have undone your selfe, and your sister, my Lady Catalina hath found it, and is mad with rage, and envy against you; I overtheard your destruction, she hath shewed it to Don Valasce, and hath plotted that he shall steale you away this night, the doores shall be lest open the houre after twelve.

BERINTHIA
You amaze me, tis impossible.

DIEGO
Doe not cast away your selfe, by incredulity, upon my life your fate is cast, nay more, worse then that.

BERINTHIA
Worse?

DIEGO
You must be poysoned too, oh shees a cunning devill, and she will carry it so, that Valasco shall bee suspected for your death, what will you doe?

BERINTHIA
I am overcome with amazement?

DIEGO
Madam remember with what noble love my Master Antonio does honour you, and now both save your selfe, and make him happy, how.

BERINTHIA
I am lost man.

DIEGO

Feare not, I will engage my life for your safety,
Seeme not to have knowledge or suspicion, be carefull
What you receive, least you be poysond, leave the
Rest to me, I have a crotchet in my pate shall spoil
Their musicke, and prevent all danger I warrant you,
By any meanes be smooth, and pleasant, the devils
A knave, your sisters a Traytor, my Master is your noble
Friend, I am your honest servant, and Valasco shall
Shake his eares like an annimall.

BERINTHIA

It is not to be hoped for.

DIEGO

Then cut of my eares, slit my nose, and make a devill of me, shall I about it say, tis done.

BERINTHIA

Any thing thou art honest, heaven be neare,
Still to my innocence, I am full of feare.

DIEGO

Spurre cut and away then.

[Exeunt

SCENE II

The Same. Sharkino's Study.

Furnished with glasses, phials, pictures of wax characters, wands, conjuring habit, poweders and paintings.

Enter Signior **SHARKINO** and **SCARABEO**.

SHARKINO

Scarabeo!

SCARABEO

Sir.

SHARKINO

Is the doore tongue tide, scrue your selfe halfe out of one of the crevices, and give me notice what patient approathes me.

SCARABEO

I can runne through the key hole sir.

[Exit.

SHARKINO
This fucus beares
A lively tincture, oh the checke mnst blush
That weares it, their deceiv'd that say
Art is the ape of nature.

SCARABEO [within]
Sir.

SHARKINO
Who ist?

SCARABEO [within]
My Ladies apronstrings, Mistris Ansilva her chambermaide.

SHARKINO
Admit her.

[Enter **ANSILVA**.

ANSILVA
How now raw head and bloody bones, wheres the
Doctor Sharkino? oh here he is.

SHARKINO
How does your vertuous Ladie.

ANSILVA
In good health sir.
Wheres the Fucus, and the Powder?

SHARKINO
All is prepared here.

ANSILVA
To see what you can doe, many make legges, and you make faces sir.

SHARKINO
Variety of faces is now in fashion, and all little enough for some to set a good face on't, oh Ladies may now and then commit a slip and have some colour for't, but these are but the outsides of our art, the things we can prescribe to be taken inwardly, are pretty curiosities, we can prolong life.

ANSILVA
And kill too can you not?

SHARKINO

Oh any that will goe to the price.

ANSILVA

You have poysons I warrant you, how doe they looke? pray lets see one.

SHARKINO

Oh naturall and artificiall, Nessas blood was milke
To em, an extraction of Todes and Vipers, looke
Heres a parcell of Claudius Caesars posset,
Given him by his wife Agrippina here is some of
Hannibals medicine he carried alwaies in the
Pummell of his sword, for a dead lift, a very active
Poyson, which passing the Orifice, kindles
Straite a fire inflames the blood, and makes the marrow
Fry, have you occasion to apply one.

ANSILVA

Introth we are troubled with a rat in my Ladies Chamber.

SHARKINO

A Rat, give him his bane, would you destroy a City, I have probatinus of Italian Sallets, and our owne Country figs shall doe it rarely, a Rat, I have scarse a poyson so base, the worst is able to kill a man, I have all sorts, from a minute to seven yeares in operation, and leave no markes behinde em, a Rats a Rat.

ANSILVA

Pray let me see a remover at twelve houres, and I would be loath to kill the poore thing presently.

SHARKINO

Here, you may cast it away upon't, but tis a disparagement to the poyson.

ANSILVA

This will content you.

[Gives him money.

SHARKINO

Because it is for a Rat you shall pay no more, my service to my Ladie,

[Exit **ANSILVA**.

My poysons howsoever I give them, variety of operations are all but one. Honest Rats bane in severall-shapes, their vertue is common, and will not be long in killing; you were best looke it be a Rat,

[Knocks within.

—Scarabeo.

[Enter **SCARABEO**.

SCARABEO
Sir heres a Gallant enquires for Dector Sharkino

SHARKINO
Usher him in, it is some Don.

[Enter **COUNT de MONTE NIGRO**.

COUNT de MONTE NIGRO
Is your name Signior Sharkino, the famous Doctor?

SHARKINO
They call me Sharkino.

COUNT de MONTE NIGRO
Doe you not know me?

SHARKINO
Your gracious pardon.

COUNT de MONTE NIGRO
I am Count de Monte Nigro.

SHARKINO
Your honours sublimity doth illustrate this habitation.
Is there any thing wherein Sharkino may expresse
His humble service? if ought within the circumference
Of a medicinall or Mathematicall science,
May have acceptance with your celsitude,
It shall devolve it selfe.

COUNT de MONTE NIGRO
Devolve it selfe, that word is not in my Table booke; what are all these trinkets?

SHARKINO
Take heed, I beseech your honour, they are dangerous, this is the devil's girdle.

COUNT de MONTE NIGRO
A pox oth devill, what have I doe with him,

SHARKINO
It is a dreadfull circle of conjuration, fortified
With sacred characters against the power
Of infernal spirits, within whose round I can tread

Safely, when hell burnes round about me.

COUNT de MONTE NIGRO
Not unlikely.

SHARKINO
Will you see the devill sir?

COUNT de MONTE NIGRO
Ha! the devil? not at this time, I am in some hast,
Any thing but the devill I durst fight with all, harke
You Doctor, letting these things passe, hearing
Of your skill, I am come in my owne person, for
A fragment of your art, harke you, have you any
Receipts to procure love sir?

SHARKINO
All the degrees of it this is ordinary.

[Shewing a phial.

COUNT de MONTE NIGRO
Nay I would not have it too strong, the Lady I intend it for, is pretty well taken already, an easing
working thing does it.

SHARKINO
Here's a powder whose ingrediences were fetchd
From Arabia the happy, a sublimation of the Phoenix
Ashes, when she last burned her selfe, it beares the
Colour of sinamon, two or three souples put into
A cup of wine, fetches up her heart, she can scarce
Keepe it in, for running out of her mouth to you
My noble Lord.

COUNT de MONTE NIGRO
That, let me have that, Doctor I know tis deare,
Will that gold buy it?

[Gives him money.

SHARKINO
Your honour is bountifull, there needs no circumstance,
Minister it by whom you please, your intention binds it to operation.

COUNT de MONTE NIGRO
So, so Catalina, I will put your mornings draught
In my pocket—

[Knocke at the doore

Doctor, I would not be seene.

SHARKINO
Please you my Lord obscure your selfe behinde these hangings then, till they be gone, Ile dispatch'em the sooner; or if your honour thinke fit, tis but clouding your person with a simple cloake of mine, and you may at pleasure passe without discovery, my Anotomy shall waite on you.

[**COUNT de MONTE NIGRO** and **SCARABEO** retire.

[Enter **THREE SERVING-MEN**.

1ˢᵗ SERVING-MAN
Prethee come backe yet.

2ⁿᵈ SERVING-MAN
Oh by any meanes goe laynes.

1ˢᵗ SERVING-MAN
Dost thou thinke it possible that any man can tell where thy things are, but he that stole 'em, hee's but a jugling imposter, a my conscience, come backe againe.

2ⁿᵈ SERVING-MAN
Nay now wee are at furthest, be not rul'd by him, I know he is a cunning man, he told me my fortune once when I was to goe a journey by water, that if I scapt drowning, I should doe well enough, and I have iiv'd ever since.

3ʳᵈ SERVING-MAN
Well I will try, I am resolv'd; stay, here hee is Pedro, you are acquainted with him, breake the ice, he is alone.

2ⁿᵈ SERVING-MAN
Blesse you Mr. Doctor; sir presuming on your Art, here is a fellow of mine, indeede the Butler, for want of a better; has lost a dozen of Dyaper spoones, and halfe a dozen of silver Napkins yesterday, they were seene by all three of us in the morning betweene sixe and seven set up, and what spirit of the Buttery hath stollen'em before eight, is invisible to our understanding.

3ʳᵈ SERVING-MAN
He hath delivered you the case right: I beseech you sir doe what you can for a servant, that is like to be in a lamentable case else, heres a gratuity.

1ˢᵗ SERVING-MAN
Now we shall see what the devill can do, hey, heres one of his spirits I thinke.

SHARKINO

Betweene seven and eight the houre; the first Luna, the second Saturne, the third Jupiter, the fourth Mars, the fifth Sol, the sixth Venus, the seven Mercury, ha! then it was stolne, Mercury is a thiefe, your goods are stolne.

3rd SERVING-MAN

Was Mercury the thiefe, pray where dwells he?

SHARKINO

Mercury is above the Moone man.

3rd SERVING-MAN

Alas sir tis a great way thither.

1st SERVING-MAN

Did not I tell you you would be gull'd.

SHARKINO

Well y'are a servant, Ile doe something for you; What will you say, if I shew you the man that stole your Spoones and Napkins presently, will that satisfie you.

3rd SERVING-MAN

Ile desire no more, oh good Mr. Doctor.

1st SERVING-MAN

If he does that, ile beleve he has cunning.

SHARKINO

Goe to, heares a glasse.

2nd SERVING-MAN

Loe you there now.

SHARKINO

Stand your backes North, and stirre not till I bid you;
What see you there?

3rd SERVING-MAN

Heres nothing.

SHARKINO

Looke agen, and marke, stand yet more North.

3rd SERVING-MAN

Now I see somebody.

1st SERVING-MAN

And I.

[The **COUNT de MONTE NIGRO** comes from behind the Hangings and muffled in a cloake steales of the Stage.

SHARKINO
Marke this fellow muffled in the cloake, he hath stolne your spoones and Napkins, does he not skulke.

1ˢᵗ SERVING-MAN
'Foote tis strange, he lookes like a theefe, this Doctor I see is cunning.

3ʳᵈ SERVING-MAN
Oh rogue how shall's come by him, oh for an Officer,

SHARKINO
Yet stirre not.

3ʳᵈ SERVING-MAN
Oh hees gone, where is he?

SHARKINO
Be not too rash, my Art tells me there is danger in't, you must be blinfold all, if you observe me not, all is to no purpose, you must not see till you be forth a doores, shut your eyes, and leade one another, when you are abroad open them and you shall see agen.

3ʳᵈ SERVING-MAN
The thiefe?

SHARKINO
The same, then use your pleasures, so, be sure you see not, conduct them Scarabeo.

[Exeunt.

[Enter a **MAID** with an urinall.

MAID
Oh Mr. Doctor I have got this opportunity to come to you, but I cannot stay, heres my water, pray sweet Mr. Doctor, tell me, I am in great feare that I have lost—

SHARKINO
What?

MAID
My maidenhead sir, you can tell by my water.

SHARKINO
Dost not thou know?

MAID

Oh I doe some what doubt my selfe, for this morning when I rose, I found a paire of breeches on my bed, and I have had a great suspition ever since, it is an evill signe they say, and one does not know what may be in those breeches sometimes; sweets Mr. Doctor, am I a maid still or no, I would be sorry to loose my maiden head ere I were aware, I feare I shall never be honest after it.

SHARKINO
Let me see urina meretrix; the colour is a strumpet, but the contents deceive not, your maiden head is gone.

MAID
And is there no hope to finde it againe?

SHARKINO
You are not every body, by my Art, as in other things that have beene stolne, he that hath stolne your maiden head shall bring it againe.

MAID
Thanke you sweet Mr. Doctor, I am in your debt for this good newes; oh sweet newes sweet Mr. Doctor.

[Exit.

[Enter **COUNT de MONTE NEGRO** beating before him the three **SERVING-MEN**, they runne in.

1ˢᵗ SERVING-MAN
Cry your honour mercy, good my Lord.

COUNT de MONTE NIGRO
Out you slaves, oh my toes.

SHARKINO
What ayles your Lordship?

COUNT de MONTE NIGRO
Doctor, I am out of breath, where be these wormes crept, I was never so abused since I was swadled: harke you; those three Rogues that were here even now, began to lay hold of me, and told me I must give them their Spoones and Napkins; they made a theefe of mee, but I thinke I have made their flesh jelly with kickes and bastinadoes; oh I have no mercy when I set on't, I have made them all poore Johns, impudent varlets; talke to me of Spoones and Napkins.

SHARKINO
Alas one of them was mad, and brought to me to cure him.

COUNT de MONTE NIGRO
Nay they were all mad, but I thinke I have madded e'm; I feare J have kickt two or three out of their lives; alas poore Wretches I am sorry for it now, but I have such an humor of beating & kicking when my footes in once: harke you Doctor, is it not within the compasse of your physicke to take downe a mans courage a thought lower; the truth is, I am apt of myselfe to quarrell upon the least affront ith' world, I cannot be kept in, chaines will not hold me: totherday for a lesse matter than this, I kickt halfe a dozen

of high Germans, from one end of the streete to the other, for but offering to shrinke betweene mee and wall; not a day goes o're my head but I hurt some body mortally; poxe a these rogues, I am sorry at my heart I have hurt e'm so, but I can not forbeare.

SHARKINO
This is strange.

COUNT de MONTE NIGRO
How? I can scarce forbeare striking you now, for saying it is strange; you would not thinke it: oh the wounds J have given for a very looke; well harke you, if it be not too late, I would be taken downe, but I feare tis impossible, and then every one goes in danger of his life by me.

SHARKINO
Take downe your spirit, looke you, dee see this inch and a halfe, how tall a man doe you thinke he was? He was twelve cubits high, and three yards compasse at the waste when I tooke him in hand first, ile draw him through a ring ere I have done with him: I keepe him now to breake my poysons, to eate Spiders and Toades, which is the onely dish his heart wishes for; a Capon destroyes him, and the very sight of beefe or mutton makes him sicke; looke, you shall see him eate his supper, come on your wayes, what say you to this Spider? looke how he leapes.

SCARABEO
Oh dainty.

SHARKINO
Here, saw you that? how many legges now for the hanch of a Toade.

SCARABEO
Twenty, and thanke you sir, oh sweete Toade, oh admirable Toade.

COUNT de MONTE NIGRO
This is very strange, I nere saw the like, I never keew Spiders and Toades were such good meates before; will he not burst now?

SHARKINO
It shall ne'er swell him, by to morrow hee shall be an inch abated, and I can with an other experiment plumpe him and highten him at my pleasure; ile warrant ile take you downe my Lord.

COUNT de MONTE NIGRO
Nay but dee here, doe I looke like a Spider-catcher, or Toade-eater.

SHARKINO
Farre be it from Shirkino, I have gentle pellets for your Lordship, shall melt in your mouth, 'and take of your valour insensibly; Lozenges that shall comfort your stomacke, and but at a weeke restraine your fury two or three thoughts; does your honour thinke I would forget my selfe, I shew you by this Rat what I can doe by Art: your Lordship shall have an easie composition, no hurt ith' world in't; here take but halfe a dozen of these going to bed, e're morning; it shall worke gently, and in the vertue appeare every day afterward.

COUNT de MONTE NIGRO
But if I find myselfe braking out into fury, I may take e'm often; heres for your pellers of Lozenges, what
rare physicke is this? Ile put it in practise presently, farewell Doctor.

[Exit.

SHARKINO
Happinesse wait on your egregious Lordship, my physicke Shall make your body soluble, but for working
on your spirit, beleeve it when you finde it; with any lies we must set forth siour'mples and compositions
to utter them: so this is a good dayes worke; leane chaps lay up, and because you have perform'd
hamsomly, there is some silver for you, lay up my properties: Tis night already, thus we knaves will
thrive, when honest plainnesse know not how to live.

[Exeunt.

SCENE III

The Same. A Room in Vilarezo's House.

[Enter **CATALINA** and **ANSILVA**.

CATALINA
Art sure she has tane it?

ANSILVA
As sure as I am alive? she never eate with
Such an appetite, for I found none left, I would
Be loath to have it so sure in my belly, it will worke
Rarely twelve houres hence.

CATALINA
Thus we worke sure then, time runnes upon
Th' appointed houre, Valasco should rid me of all my
Feares at once, upon thy life be carefull to direct
Him at his first approach, I am sicke till she
Be delivered; be secret as the night, ile to my
Chamber, be very carefull.

SCENE IV

The Same. A Garden Behind Vilarezo's House.

[Enter **ANTONIO**, **VILLANDRAS**, **DIEGO**, vizarded and arm'd.

ANTONIO

Art sure thou hast the time right.

DIEGO

Doubt not, yonder's her chamber, the light speakes it; softly.

ANSILVA

Whose there? Vallasco?

ANTONIO

I.

ANSILVA

That way, make no noise, things are prepared, softly
So, so, this is good I hope and weight too, my Lady
Berinthia will be sure enough anon, I shall nere
Get more higher, I had much adoe to perswade her
To the spice, but I swore it was a cordiall my Lady
Vs'd her selfe, and poore foole she has swallowed it
Sure.

[Exit.

SCENE V

The Same.

[Enter **ANTONIO** with **BERINTHIA, VILLANDRAS, DIEGO**.

ANTONIO

Madam feare not I am your friend.

BERINTHIA

Who are you?

VILLANDRAS

Stop her mouth, away!

[Exeunt.

SCENE VI

The Same.

[Enter **ANSILVA**.

ANSILVA
So, so, they are gone, alas poore Valasco I pitty thee,
But we creatures of polliticke Ladies must hold the
Same byas with our Mistresses, and tis some pollicy
To make them respect us the better, for feare our
Teeth be not strong enough to keepe in our tongues:
Now must I study out some tale by morning to salute
My old Lord withall.

[Enter **VALASCO**, with two **FRIENDS** armed.

VALASCO
Ansilva!

ANSILVA
Some body calls me, who is it?

VALASCO
It is I Valasco

ANSILVA
What comes he backe for? I hope the poyson does
Not worke already, where have you dispos'd her.

VALASCO
Dispos'd whom?

ANSILVA
My Lady Berinthia.

VALASCO
Let me alone to dispose her, prethee where's the light?
Shew us the way.

ANSILVA
What way?

VALASCO
The way to her chamber? come, I know what
You are sicke of—

[Gives her money.

Here each minute is an age till
I possesse Berinthia.

ANSILVA
This is pretty, I hope my lady is well.

VALASCO
Well?

ANSILVA
My Lady Berinthia sir.

VALASCO
Doe you mocke me?

ANSILVA
I mocke you?

VALASCO
I shall grow angry, lead me to
Berinthias chamber, or—

ANSILVA
Why sir, were not you here even now, and hurried
Her away, I have your gold well fare all good tokens;
I have perform'd my duty already sir, and you had my
Lady.

VALASCO
I am abus'd you are a cunning Devill, I heare and had
Berinthia, tell me, or with this pistoll, I will soone
Reward thy treachery, where Berinthia?

ANSILVA
Oh I beseech you doe not fright me so, if you were
Not here even now, here was another that call'd
Himselfe Valasco, to whom I gave accesse, and
He has carried her away.

[Exit.

VALASCO
Am I awake? or doe I dreame this horrour:
Where am I? who does know me, are you friends
Of Don Valasco?

1ˢᵗ FRIEND
Doe you doubt us sir?

VALASCO

I doubt my selfe, who am I

2nd FRIEND
Our noble friend Valasco,

VALASCO
Tis so, I am Valasco, all the Furies
Circle me round, oh teach me to be mad,
I am abus'd, infufferably tormented,
My very soule is whipt, it had beene safer
For Catalina to have plaid with Serpents.

[Enter **CATALINA** and **ANSILVA**.

CATALINA
Thou talkest of wonders, where is Valasco?

ANSILVA
He was here even now.

VALASCO
Who nam'd Valasco?

CATALINA
Twas I, Catalina, here.

VALASCO
Could you picke none out of the stocke of man
To mocke but me, so basely?

CATALINA
Valasco be your selfe, resume your vertue.
My thoughts are cleare from your abuse, it is
No time to vent our passions, fruitlesse rages,
Some hath abus'd us both, but a revenge
As swift as lightning shall pursue their flight:
Oh I could feare my braines, as you respect
Your honoures safety, or Berinthias love;
Haste to your lodging, which being nere our house,
You shall be sent for; seeme to be rais'd up,
Let us alone to make a noise at home,
Fearefull as thunder; try the event, this cannot
Doe any hurt, you Ansilva shall
With clamors wake the houshold cunningly,
While I prepare my selfe.

VALASCO
I will suspend awhile.

[*Exeunt* all but **ANSILVA**.

ANSILVA
Help! Help! Thieves! Villains! Murder! my Lady!
Helpe oh my Lord, my Lady, murder theeves helpe.

[*Enter* **SEBASTIANO** *in his shirt with a Taper.*

SEBESTIANO
What fearefull cry is this, where are you?

ANSILVA
Here oh I am almost kil'd.

SEBESTIANO
Ansilva where art hurt?

ANSILVA
All over sir, my Lady Berinthia is carried away
By Ruffians, that broke into her chamber, alas
Sees gone.

SEBESTIANO
Whether? which way?

[*Enter* **GASPAR DE VILAREZO** *and* **CATALINA**.

My sister Berinthia is violently tane out of her
Chamber, and heres Ansilva hurt, see looke about,
Berinthia sister.

CATALINA
How Berinthia gone? Call up the servants.
Ansilva, how wast?

ANSILVA
Alas Madam, I have not my senses about me, I am so
Frighted, vizards, and swords, and pistols, but my
Lady Berinthia was quickly seiz'd upon, shees gone.

GASPAR DE VILAREZO
What villaines durst attempt it?

[*Enter* **COUNT de MONTE NIGRO** *with a torch.*

I feare Valasco guilty of this rape.

CATALINA
Runne one to his lodging presently, it will appeare
I know he lov'd her, oh my Lord, my sister Berinthias lost,

COUNT de MONTE NIGRO
How? foote my physicke begins to worke, ile come to you presently.

[Exit.

CATALINA
Wheres Diego? he is missing, runne one to his chamber, heres Valasco.

[Enter **VALASCO**.

SEBESTIANO
It is apparant sir, Valascoes noble.

CATALINA
Berinthias stolen away.

VALASCO
Ha!

SEBESTIANO
Her Chamber broken ope, and shee ta'en thence this night.

VALASCO
Confusion stay the thief!.

[Enter **COUNT de MONTE NIGRO**.

COUNT de MOUNTE NIGRO
So, so, as you were saying, Berinthia was stolene away by some body, and—

[Enter **SERVANT**

1st SERVANT
Diego is not in his chamber.

CATALINA
Didst breake ope the doore?

1st SERVANT
I did, and found all empty.

COUNT de MONTE NIGRO

How, Diego gone? thats strange, oh it workers againe, Ile come to you presently.

[Exit

CATALINA
I doe suspect—
This some plot of Antonio,
Diego, a subtle villaine,
Confirmes himselfe an instrument by this absence;
What thinkest Ansilva?

ANSILVA
Indeed I heard some of them name Antonio.

VILLANDRAS, CATALINA, SEBESTIANO
Ha!

VILLANDRAS
Tis true upon my soule, oh false Antonio.

CATALINA
Unworthy Gentleman.

VALASCO
Let none have the honour to revenge, but I the wrongd
Valasco, let me beg it sir.

GASPAR DE VILAREZO
Antonio, boy up before the day,
Vpon my blessing I command thee post
To Eluas Castle, summon that false man

[Enter **COUNT de MONTE NIGRO**

To quit his shamefull action, bid him returne
Thy sister backe, whose honour will be lost
For ever in't, if he shall dare deny her,
Double thy Fathers spirit, call him to
A strickt account, and with thy sword enforce him,
Oh I could leape out of my age me thinkes,
And combat him my selfe; be thine the glory,
This staine will never wash off, I feele it settle
On all our blood, away, my curse pursue
This disobedience.

[Exit

VALASCO
I had an interrest in Berinthia,
Why have not I commission, I have a sword,
Thirsleth to be acquainted with his veines;
It is too meane a satisfaction
To have her rendred, on his heart Ide write
A most just vengence.

SEBESTIANO
Sir she is my sister, I have a sword dares tent
A wound as farre as any; spare your vallour

CATALINA
I have a tricke to be rid of this foole, my Lord
[To **COUNT de MONTE NIGRO**]
Doe you accompany my brother, you
I know are valiant.

COUNT de MONTE NIGRO
Any whither, Ile make me ready presently.

[Exit

SEBESTIANO
My most unhappy sister.

[Exit

CATALINA
Oh I could surfet, I am confident
Antonio hath her, tis revenge beyond
My expectation, to close up the eyes
Of his Berinthia, dying in his armes,
Poyson'd maturely, mischiefe I shall prove
Thy constant friend, let weakenesse vertue love.

[Exeunt **CATALINA** and **ANSILVA**.

ACTUS IV

SCENE I

Elvas. A Room in the Castle.

Enter **ANTONIO, BERINTHIA, CASTABELLA, VILLANDRAS, SFORZA, DIEGO.**

ANTONIO

The welcom'st guest that ever Eluas had
Sister, Villandras yare not sensible what treasure
You possesse, I have no loves, I would not here divide.

CASTABELLA

Indeed Madam, yare as welcome here, as are my mother was.

GASPAR DE VILAREZO

And you are here as safe, as if you had an army for your Guard.

SFORZA

Safe armies, and guard! Berinthia you're a Lady,
But I meane not to court you: guard quotha, here's
A Toledo, and an old arme, tough bones and sinewes,
Able to cut off as stout a head as wags upon a shoulder,
Thart Antonios guest, welcome by the old bones
Of his Father, th'ast a wall of brass about thee
My young Daffodill.

GASPAR DE VILAREZO

Nor thinke my noble cousin meaneth you any dishonour here.

ANTONIO

Dishonour, it is a language I never understood, yet
Throw off your feares Berinthia, yare ith' power
Of him that dares not thinke
The least dishonour to you.

SFORZA

True by this busse jerkin, that hath look'd ith face of an Army, and he lies like a termagant, denies it,
Antonio is Lord of the Castle, but ile command fire to the gunnes, upon any Renegado that confronts us,
set thy heart at rest my gilloflower, we are all friends I warrant thee, and hees a Turke that does not
honour thee from the haire of thy head, to thy pettitoes.

ANTONIO

Come be not sad.

CASTABELLA

Put on fresh blood, yare not cheerefull, how doe you?

BERINTHIA

I know not how, nor what to answer you,
Your loves I cannot be ungratefull to,
Yare my best friends I thinke, but yet I know not
With what consent you brought my body hither.

ANTONIO
Can you be ignorant what plot was laid
To take your faire life from you.

BERINTHIA
If all be not a dreame, I doe remember
Your servant Diego told me wenders, and
I owe you for my preservation, but—

SFORZA
Shoot not at Buts, Cupids an atcher, here a faire marke, a fool's bolts soone shot, my names Sforza still,
my double Daisie.

CASTABELLA
It is your happinesse you have escaped the malice of your sister.

GASPAR DE VILAREZO
And it is worth
A noble gratitude to have been quit,
By such an honourer as Antonio is
Of faire Berinthia.

BERINTHIA
Oh but my Father, under whose displeasure I ever sinke,

ANTONIO
You are secure

BERINTHIA
As the poore Deere that being pursuid, for safety
Gets up a rocke that over hangs the Sea,
Where all that she can see, is her destruction,
Before the waves, behinde her enemies
Promise her certaine ruine.

ANTONIO
Faine not your selfe so haplesse my Berinthia,
Ralse your dejected thoughts, be merry, come,
Thinke I am your Antonio.

CASTABELLA
It is not wisdome
To let our passed fortune, trouble us,
Since were they bad the memorie is sweete,
That we have past them, looke before you Lady,
The future most concerneth.

BERINTHIA
You have awak'd me, Antonio pardon,
Upon whose honour I dare trust my selfe,
I am resolv'd if you dare keepe me here,
T'expect some happier issue.

ANTONIO
Dare keepe thee here? with thy consent, I dare
Deny thy Father, by this sword I dare,
And all the world.

SFORZA
Dare, what giant of vallour dates hinder us, from daring to slit the weasands of them that dare say, wee dare not doe any thing, that is to be dared under the poles, I am old Sforza, that in my dayes have scoured rogues faces with hot bals, made em cut crosse capers, and sent them away with a powder, I have a company of roring buls upon the wals, shall spit fire in the faces of any ragamuffian that dares say, we dare not fight pell mell, and still my name is Sforza.

[Enter **DIEGO** hastily.

DIEGO
Sir your noble friend don Sebastionc is at the castle gate

ANTONIO
Your brother Lady, and my honoured friend,
Why doe the gates not spread themselves, to open
At his arrivall Sforza, tis Berinthiaes brother,
Sebastiano the example of all worth
And friendship, is come after his sweete sister,

BERINTHIA
Alas I feare.

ANTONIO
Be not such a coward Lady, he cannot come
Without all goodnesse waiting on him, Sforza,
Sforza I say, what pretious time we lose,
Sebastiano, I almost lose my selfe
In joy to meete him, breake the iron bars
And give him entrance.

SFORZA
Ile breake the wals downe, if the gates be too little.

CASTABELLA
I much desire to see him.

ANTONIO
Sister, now hees come, he did promise me
But a short absence, he of all the world
I would call brother, Castabella more
Then for his sisters love, oh hees a man
Made up of merit, my Berinthia
Throw off all cloudes, Sebastianoes come.

BERINTHIA
Sent by my Father to—

ANTONIO
What, to see thee? he shall see thēe hēre.
Respected like thy selfe, Berinthia,
Attended with Antonio, begirt with armies of thy servants

[Enter **SEBASTIANO, COUNT de MONTE NIGRO, SFORZA.**

Oh my friend.

SEBESTIANO
'Tis yet in question sir, and will not be
So easily proved.

COUNT de MONTE NIGRO
No sir, weele make you prove your selfe our friend.

ANTONIO
What face have you put on? am I awake?
Or doe I dreame Sebastiano frownes.

SEBESTIANO
Antonio I come not now to Complement,
While you were noble, I was not least of them
You cald your friends, but you are guilty of
An action that destroyes that name.

SFORZA
Bones o' your Father, does he come to swagger,
My name is Sforza then.

ANTONIO
No more,
I guiltie of an action so dishonourable
Has made me unworthy of your friendship;
Come y'are not in earnest, tis enough I know

My se'fe Antonio.

SEBESTIANO
Adde to him ungratefull.

ANTONIO
Twas a foule breath delivered it, and wert any
But Sebastiano, he should feele the weight
Of such a falshood.

SEBESTIANO
Sister you must along with me.

ANTONIO
Now by my Fathers soule, he that takes her hence
Vnlesse she give consent, treads on his grave,
Sebastiano, y'are unnoble then,
Tis I that said it.

COUNT de MOUNTE NIGRO
So it seemes.

SEBESTIANO
Antonio, for here I throw of all
The ties of love, I come to fetch a sister,
Dishonourably taken from her father;
Or with my sword to force thee render her:
Now if thou beest a Souldier redeliver,
Or keepe her with the danger of thy person,
Thou canst not be my brother, till we first
Be allied in blood.

ANTONIO
Promise me the hearing,
And shalt have any satisfaction,
Becomes my fame.

COUNT de MOUNTE NIGRO
So, so, he will submit himselfe, it will be our honor.

ANTONIO
Were in your power, would you not account it
A pretious victory, in your sisters cause,
To dye your sword with any blood of him,
Sav'd both her life and honour?

SEBESTIANO

I were ungratefull.

ANTONIO

You have told your selfe, and I have argumēnt to prove this.

SEBESTIANO

Why would you have me thinke, my sister owes to you such preservation?

ANTONIO

Oh Sebastiano,
Thou dost not thinke what devill lies at home
Within a sisters bosome, Catalina,
(I know not with what worst of envy) laid
Force to this goodly building, and through poyson
Had rob'd the earth of more then all the world,
Her vertue.

SEBESTIANO

You must not beate my resolution off
With these inventions sir.

ANTONIO

Be not cozend,
With your credulity, for my blood, I value it
Beneath my honour, and I dare by goodnesse,
In such a quarrell kill thee: but heare all,
And then you shall have fighting your heart full.
Valasco was the man, appointed by
That goodly sister to steale Berinthia,
And Lord himselfe of this possession,
Just at that time; but heare and tremble at it,
Shee by a cunning poyson should have breath'd
Her soule into his armes, within two houres,
And so Valasco should have borne the shame
Of thest and murther; how doe you like this sir.

SEBESTIANO

You amaze me sir.

ANTONIO

Tis true by honours selfe, heare it confirm'd,
And when you will, I am ready.

GASPAR DE VILAREZO

Pitty such valour should be imployd,

Vpon no better cause, they will enforme him.

COUNT de MONTE NIGRO
Harke you sir, dee thinke this is true?

GASPAR DE VILAREZO
I dare maintaine it.

COUNT de MONTE NIGRO
Thats another matter, why then the case is
Altered, what should we doe fighting, and lose
Our lives to no purpose.

SFORZA
It seemes you are his second.

MOUNTE NIGRO
I am Count de Monte Nigro.

SFORZA
And my names Sforza sir, you were not best to come here to brave us, unlesse you have more legges
and armes at home, I have a saza shall picke holes in your doublet, and firke your shankes, my
gallimaufry.

SEBESTIANO
I cannot but beleeve it, oh Berinthia,
I am wounded ere I fight.

ANTONIO
Holds your resolve yet constant? if you have
Better opinion of your sword, then truth,
I am bound to answer, but I would I had
Such an advantage gainst another man,
As the justice of my cause, all vallour fights
But with a sayle against it.

GASPAR DE VILAREZO
Take a time to informe your father sir, my noble
Cozen is to be found here constant.

SEBESTIANO
But will you backe with me then?

BERINTHIA
Excuse me brother, I shall fall too soone
Vpon my sisters malice, whose foule guilt
Will make me expect more certaine ruine,

ANTONIO
Now Sebestiano
Puts on his judgement, and assumes his noblenesse,
Whilst he loves equity.

SEBESTIANO
And shall I carry shame
To Villarezoes house, neglect of father,
Whose precepts bindes me to returne with her,
Or leave my life at Eluas, I must on,
I have heard you to no purpose, shall Berinthia
Backe to Avero.

ANTONIO
Sir she must not yet, tis dangerous.

SEBESTIANO
Choose thee a second then, this Count and
Meane to leave honor here.

VILLANDRAS
Honour me sir.

ANTONIO
'Tis done, Sebastiano shall report
Antonio just and noble, Sforza sweare
Vpon my Sword, oh doe not hinder me
If victory crowne Sebastianoes arme.
I charge thee by thy honesty restore
This Lady to him, on whose lip I seale
My unstain'd faith.

COUNT de MONTE NIGRO
Umph, tis a rare physician, my spirit is abated.

CASTABELLA
Brother.

BERINTHIA
Brother.

SEBESTIANO
And wilt thou be dishonourd?

BERINTHIA
Oh doe not wrong the Gentleman, beleeve it

Dishonour nere dwelt here, and he hath made
A most religious vow, not in a thought
To staine my innocence, he does not force me
Remember, what a noble friend, you make
A most just enemy, he sav'd my life,
Be not a murtherer, take yet a time,
Runne not your selfe in danger for a cause
Carries so little justice.

COUNT de MONTE NIGRO
Faith sir, if you please take a time to thinke on't, a month or two or three, they shall not say but wee are honorable.

[**SEBASTIANO** whispers to **COUNT de MONTE NEGRO**.

CASTABELLA
You gave him to my heart a Gentleman, Seb whisp.
Compleate with goodnesse, will you rob the world
And me at once, alas I love him.

ANTONIO
Never man fought with a lesser heart, the conquest
Will be but many deathes, he is her brother,
My friend, this poore girles joy.

COUNT de MONTE NIGRO
With all my heart, Ile post to Avero presently.

SEBESTIANO
Let it be so Antonio.

CASTABELLA
Alas pore Castabella, what a conflict
Feest thou within thee, their fight woundeth thee,
And I must die, who ere hath victory:

ANTONIO
Then friend againe, and as Sebastiano,
I bid him welcome, and who loves Antonio
Must speake that language.

SFORZA
Enough, not a Masty upon the Castle wall
But shall barke too, I congratulate thee, if thou
Beelest friend to the Castle of Eluas, and still my name
Is Sforza.

ANTONIO
Well said my brave Adelautado, come Sebastiano,
And my Birinthia by to morrow we shall know
The truth of our felicity.

[Exeunt.

SCENE II

Avero. A Room in Vilarezo's House.

[Enter **GASPAR de VILAREZO**.

GASPAR DE VILAREZO
What are the Nobles more than common men
When all their honour cannot free them from
Shame and abuse; as greatnesse were a marke
Stucke by them but to give direction
For men to shoote indignities upon them?
Are we call'd Lords of riches we possesse,
And can defend them from the ravishing hand
Of strangers, when our children are not safe
From theeves and robbers, none of us can challenge
Such right to wealth and fortuues of the world,
Being things without us; but our children are
Essentiall to us, and participate
Of what we are: part of our very nature,
Our selves but cast into a younger mold,
And can we promise, but so weake assurance
Of so neere treasures. O Villarezo shall
Thy age be trampled on, no, it shall not,
I will be knowne a father, Portugall
Shall not report this infamy unreveng'd,
It will be a barre in Vilarezo's armes
Past all posterity;

[Enter **CATALINA**.

Come Catalina, thou wilt stay with me,
Prepare to welcome home Sebastiano,
Whom I expect with honour, and that baggage
Ambitious girle Berinthia.

CATALINA
Alas sir; censure not her too soone,

Till she appeare are guilty.

GASPAR DE VILAREZO
Heres thy vertue still,
To excuse her Catalina, no beleeve it,
Shes naught, past hope, I have an eye can see
Into her very heart, thou art too innocent.

[Enter **VALASCO**.

Valasco welcome too, Berinthia
Is not come home yet, but we shall seē her
Brought backe with shame; and ist not justice Ha!
What can be shame enough?

VALASCO
Your daughter sir?

GASPAR DE VILAREZO
My daughter? doe not call her so, she has not
True blood of Vilarezo in her veines;
She makes her selfe a bastard, and deserves
To be cut off like a disordered branch,
Disgracing the faire tree she springeth from.

VALASCO
Lay not so great a bourthen on Berinthia,
Her nature knowes not to degenerate;
Upon my life she was not yeelding, to
The injurious action; if Antonio
Have plaied the theefe, let your revenge fall there,
Which were I trusted with, although I doubt not
Sebastiano's fury; he should feele it
More heavy than his Castle, what can be
Too just for such a sinne?

GASPAR DE VILAREZO
Right, right Valasco, I doe love thee fort,
Tis so, and thou shalt see I have a sence
Worthy my birth and person.

VALASCO
'T will become you; but I marvell we hearē nothing
Of their successe at Elvas. by this time
I would have sent Antonio to warme
His fathers ashes, doe you not thinke sir?
Sebastiano will not be remisse,

A gentle nature is abus'd with tales,
Which they know how to colour; heres the Count.

[Enter **COUNT de MONTE NIGRO** sweating.

CATALINA
How, the Count? I sent him thither to be rid on him;
The foole has better fortune than I wisht him,
But now I shall heare that which will more comfort me,
My sisters death most certainely.

COUNT de MONTE NIGRO
My Lord, I have rid hard, read there—

[Delivers a letter.

Your sonne
And daughter is well.

CATALINA [aside]
Ha! well?

COUNT de MONTE NIGRO
Madam.

CATALINA
How does my sister?

COUNT de MONTE NIGRO
In good health, she has commendations to you
In that letter.

VALASCO
And is Antonio living?

COUNT de MONTE NIGRO
Yes, and remembers his service to you,

VALASCO
Has he then yielded up Berinthia?

COUNT de MONTE NIGRO
He will yeeld up his ghost first, I know not we were
Going to flesh baste one another, I am sure but the
Matter of fellony hangs still, who will cut it downe;
I know not, Madam theres notable matter against you.

CATALINA

Me?

COUNT de MONTE NIGRO
Upon my honor there is, be not angry with me,
No lesse than theft and murder, that letter is charg'd
Withall, but you'le cleare all I make no question, they Talke of poysoning.

CATALINA [aside]
Am I betray'd?

COUNT de MONTE NIGRO
Well, I smell, I smell.

CATALINA
What do you smell?

COUNT de MONTE NIGRO
It was but a tricke of theirs to save their lives,
For we were bent to kill all that came against us.

GASPAR DE VILAREZO
Catalina reade here, Valasco, both of you—

[Gives them the letter.

—And let me reade your faces, Ha! they wonder.

VALASCO
How's this, I steal Berinthia?

CATALINA
I poyson my sister.

VALASCO
This doth amaze me.

CATALINA
Father, this letter sayes I would have poysoned my poore sister, innocence defend me.

GASPAR DE VILAREZO
It will, it shall, come Jacquit you both,
They must not thus foole me.

COUNT de MONTE NIGRO
Madam I thought as much, my minde gave me, it
Was a lie, yes, you looke like a poysoner, as much
As I looke like a Hobby-horse.

CATALINA
Was ever honest love so abused, have I
So poore reward for my affection.

GASPAR DE VILAREZO
It shall be so.

[Exit.

VALASCO [aside to **CATALINA**]
Madam I know not how the poyson came in, but I
Feare some have betraied our plot.

CATALINA
And how came you off my noble Count.

COUNT de MONTE NIGRO
As you see without any wounds, but much against
My will I was but one, Sebastiano, that was the
Principall, tooke a demurre upon their allegation:
It seemes, and so the matter is rak'd up in the Embers.

VALASCO
To make a greater fire, were you so cold
To credit his excuse, Antonio,
I should not have beene so frozen,
As you love honor and revenge, give me
Some interest now, and if I doe not
Shew my selfe faithfull, let Valasco have
No name within your memory, let me begge
To be your Proxie sir, pitty such blood,
As yours should be ignobly cast away;
Maddam speake for me.

CATALINA [aside]
No, I had rather lost this foole.

COUNT de MONTE NIGRO
And you can get their consents.

CATALINA
You cannot sir in honour now goe backe.
I shall not thinke you love me, if my father
Point you such noble service to refuse it.

[Enter **GASPAR DE VILAREZO**.

COUNT de MONTE NIGRO
You heare what she sayes.

GASPAR DE VILAREZO
Count de Monte Nigro.

VALASCO
I am all fire with rage.

GASPAR DE VILAREZO
Valasco, you may accompany the Count,
There may be imployment of your valour too;
Tell me at your returne, whether my sonne
May prove a souldier, heres new warrant for
Antonioes death—

[Gives him a letter.

If there be coldnesse urge it,
Tis my desire, ile study a better service.

VALASCO
I shall.

GASPAR DE VILAREZO
Away then both, no complement, I wish you either
Had a Pegasus, be happy, my old bloud boyles, this
Must my peace secure, such sores as these must
Have a desperate cure.

[Exeunt.

SCENE III

Elvas. A Room in the Castle. A Banquet Set Out.

[Enter **SEBASTIANO, CASTABELLA. ANTONIO, BERINTHIA.**

SEBESTIANO
This honor Madam of your selfe and brother,
Make me unhappy, when I remember, what
I came for, not to feast thus but to fight.

CASTABELLA

Pitty true friendship should thus suffer.

[Music within.

ANTONIO
Ha!

SEBESTIANO
Musicke!

ANTONIO
Some conceit of Sforza the old Captaine;
Lets entertaine it, some souldiers device.

[Enter a masque of **SOULDIERS**, and dance; after which **SFORZA** enters.

SFORZA
To your stations now my brave brats of Millitary
Discipline, enough, Sforza honours you, looke to your
Charge Bullies, and be ready upon all occasions,
My invincible dub a dub knights of the Castle,
Qui vala.

[Exeunt **SOULDIERS**.

[Enter **COUNT de MONTE NIGRO, VALASCO**.

VALASCO
We must speake with Don Sebastiano.

SFORZA
Must? Th'art a Mushrumpe, mustin the Castle of Elvas?

[**COUNT de MONTE NIGRO** gives **SEBASTIANO** a letter.

ANTONIO
Friends, Sforza.

VALASCO
What, courting Ladies, by this time 'twas expected
You would have courted fame sir, and woed her to you;
You shall know me better [To **ANTONIO**].

ANTONIO
I doubt you'le never be better, you shall now owe me
More than you shall account for.

SEBESTIANO
Or else my curse, that word cries out for death.

CASTABELLA
My feates perplexe me.

[**ANTONIO** & **SEBASTIANO** whisper.

VALASCO
Madam I doe wonder
You can forget your honour, and reslect
On such unworthinesse, wherein hath Valasco
Shewed you lesse merit.

BERINTHIA
Sir it becomes not me
To weigh your worths, nor would I learne of you
How to preserve my honour.

SEBESTIANO
Sister.

ANTONIO
Villandras.

SEBESTIANO
Then I must take my leave, for I am sent for,
I am sorry for your fate, Madam I am exepected
By a father your vertue hath made me yours.

COUNT de MONTE NIGRO
Oh, admirable physician!

ANTONIO
Sfora, there is no remedie, but by all honour doe it,
Sister, I am to waite on him, oh my poore girle
Berinthia, be with thee! for a little time
Excuse my absence.

SFORZA
You may walk, sir.

VALASCO
Antonio I must but now looke on, you were
Best take a course not to out live him.

[Exeunt.

SCENE IV

The Same. A Space Outside the Castle.

Enter **ANTONIO**, **SEBASTIANO**, **VILLANDRAS** and **COUNT de MONTE NEGRO.**

ANTONIO
Sebastiano I know not with what soule
I draw my sword against thee

SEBASTIANO
Antonio I am driven in a storme
To split my selfe on thee, if not, any curse—
We must on sir.

[They fight.

COUNT de MONTE NIGRO
Rare man of art Sharkino.

VILLANDRAS
Guard thee

[**COUNT de MONTE NIGRO** and **VILLANDRAS** fight.

[Enter **SFORZA, VALASCO** and **LADIES** above.

CASTABELLA
Treacherous Sforza, hast thou brought us hither, to be stroke dead?

COUNT de MONTE NIGRO
Hold Gentlemen, give me audience.

SEBESTIANO
Whats the matter my Lord.

COUNT de MONTE NIGRO
My fit is on m; 'tis so, I had forgot my selfe,
This is my ague day.

SEBESTIANO
How?

COUNT de MONTE NIGRO
Yes a sextile ague, looke you, doe you not see me shake?
Admirable Doctor, it will be as much as my life is worth
If I should fight a stroke.

SEBESTIANO
Hell on such baseness!
We'll engage no more;
Let our words try it out.

VALASCO
Sebastiano hold, thart not so ill be friended,
Exchange a person, ile leape the battlement.

COUNT de MONTE NIGRO
Withall my heart, I am sorry it happens so unfortunately, oh rare physician!

VILLANDRAS
Good cousin, grant it.

COUNT de MONTE NIGRO
What say Sebastiano?

VILLANDRAS
I conjure you by all honour.

SEBESTIANO
It is granted;

BERINTHIA
He shall nor goe.

[Exit above **VALASCO**.

ANTONIO
Meete him my Lord, you will become his place
Of a spectator best.

[Exit **COUNT de MONTE NIGRO**.

[**SEBASTIANO** and **ANTIONIO** fight again.

BERINTHIA
Sebastiano! Brother!

[Enter **VALASCO**, below.

CASTABELLA
Antonio, here me.

GASPAR DE VILAREZO
Guard thee, Valasco then.

[They fight.

CASTABELLA
O, brother spare him for my sake.

BERINTHIA
Sebastiano every wound thou givest him,
Drawes blood from me.

CASTABELLA
Sebastiano, remember hees thy friend.

BERINTHIA
Antonio tis my brother, with whose blood
Thou dyest thy sword.

[**VALASCO** runs at **ANTONIO**.

ANTONIO
When thou liv'st againe shalt be more honorable

[Kills **VALASCO**.

Sebastiano doe you observe the advantage,
Yet thinke upon't.

SEBESTIANO
It is not in my power. I value not the odds.

[Fights with **ANTONIO** and **VILLANDRAS**.

BERINTHIA
Hold, Antonio, is this thy love to me, it is not noble.

SEBESTIANO
So thy death makes the scale even.

[Kills **VILLANDRAS**.

CASTABELLA
Antonio hold! Berinthia dyes.

BERINTHIA
Sebastiano! Castabella sinkes for sorrow. Murder! Help!
I will leape downe.

[**ANTONIO** falls.

ANTONIO
Where art Berinthia? let me breath my last upon thy lip, make haste, least I die else.

[Exeunt above, **BERINTHIA**, **CASTABELLA**, **SFORZA** and **COUNT de MONTE NIGRO**.

SEBESTIANO
Antonio, before thou dyest cut off my hand, art wounded mortally?

ANTONIO
To die by thee is more then death—Sforza be honest,
But love thy sister for me, I'm past hope,
Thou hast undone another in my death.

[Enter **BERINTHIA**, **SFORZA**, **COUNT de MONTE NIGRO**

BERINTHIA
Antonio, stay oh cruel brother!

ANTONIO
Berinthia thy lip:
Farewell, and friend, and all the world!

[Dies.

SFORZA
The gate is open, I am sworne to render.

BERINTHIA
He's not dead, his lips are warme, have you no balsom? a Surgeon—dead? Some charitable hand send my soule after him.

SEBESTIANO
Away, away!

BERINTHIA
It will be easie to die,
All life is but a walke in misery.

[Exeunt.

SCENE I

Avero. A Room in Vilarezo's House.

Enter **SEBASTIANO**.

SEBESTIANO
My friend, my noble friend, that had deserved
Most honorably from me, by this hand
Divorc'd from life, and yet I have the use ont,
Haplesle Sebastiano; oh Berinthia,
Let me for ever lose the name of Brother,
Wilt thou not curse my memory, give me up
To thy just hate a murtherer.

[Enter **GASPAR de VILAREZO**.

GASPAR DE VILAREZO
Ha, this must not be Sebastiano,
I shall be angry if you throw not off
This mellancholly, it does ill become you,
Doe you repent your duty, were the action
Againe presented to be done by thee:
And being done, againe should challenge from thee
A new performance, thou wouldst shew no blood
Of Vilarezoes, if thou didst not runne
To act it, though all horror, death and vengeance
Dog'd thee at thy heeles; come I am thy Father,
Value my blessing, and for other peace
Ile to the King, let me no more see thee cloudy.

[Exit

[Enter **DIEGO** and **CASTABELLA** dressed like a Page.

DIEGO
That was his Father.

CASTABELLA
No more, farewell: be all silence.

[Exit **DIEGO**.

CASTABELLA
Sir.

SEBESTIANO
He's newly gone that way, mayst soone ore take him

CASTABELLA
My businesse points at you sir.

SEBESTIANO
At me? What newes? thou hast a face of horrour, more welcome speake it.

CASTABELLA
If your name be Don Sebastiano, sir
I have a token from a friend.

SEBESTIANO
I have no friend alive boy, carry it backe,
Tis not to me, I've not another friend
In all the world.

CASTABELLA
He that hath sent you sir this gift, did love you,
Youle say your selfe he did.

SEBESTIANO
Ha! Name him prethee.

CASTABELLA
The friend I came from was Antonio.

SEBESTIANO
Thou lyest, and thart a villane, who hath sent thee
To tempt Sebastianoes soule to act on thee
Another death, for thus afrighting me.

CASTABELLA
Indeede I doe not mocke, nor come to afright you
Heaven knowes my heart, I know Antonioes dead,
But twas a gift he in his life design'd
To you, and I have brought it.

SEBESTIANO
Thou dost not promise cozenage, what gift is it?

CASTABELLA
It is my selfe sir, while Antonio liv'd, I was his boy,

But never did boy loose so kinde a Master, in his life he
Promised he would bestow me, so much was his love
To my poore merit, on his dearest friend,
And nam'd you sir, if heaven should point you out
To overlive him, for he knew you would
Love me the better for his sake, indeed
I will be very honest to you, and
Refuse no service to procure your love
And good opinion to me.

SEBESTIANO

Can it be
Thou wert his boy, oh thou shouldst hate me then,
Th'art false, I dare not trust thee, unto him
Thou shewest thee now unfaithfull to accept
Of me, I kild him thy Master, twas a friend
he could commit thee to, I onely was,
Of all the stocke of men his enemy,
His cruellest enemy.

CASTABELLA

Indeede I am sure it was, he spoke all truth,
And had he liv'd to have made his will, I know
He had bequeathed me as a legacy
To be your boy; alas I am willing sir
To obey him in it, had he laid on me
Command, to have mingled with his sacred dust,
My unprofitable blood, it should have beene
A most glad sacrifice, and 'thad beene honour
To have done him such a duty sir, I know
You did not kill him with a heart of mallice,
But in contention with your very soule
To part with him.

SEBESTIANO

All is as true as Oracle by heaven,
Dost thou beleeve so?

CASTABELLA

Indeede I doe.

SEBESTIANO

Yet be not rash;
Tis no advantage to belong to me,
I have no power nor greatnesse in the Court,
To raise thee to a fortune, worthy of
So much observance as I shall expect

when thou art mine.

CASTABELLA
All the ambition of my thoughts shall be
To doe my dutie sir.

SEBESTIANO
Besides, I shall afflict thy tendernesse
With sollitude and passion, for I am
Onely in love with sorrow, never merry,
Weare out the day in telling of sad tales,
Delight in sighes and teares; sometimes I walke
To a Wood or River purposely to challenge
The bouldest Eccho, to send backe my groanes
Ith' height I breake e'm, come I shall undoe thee.

CASTABELLA
Sir, I shall be most happy to beare part
In any of your sorrowes, I nere had
So hard a heart but I could shed a teare
To beare my Master company.

SEBESTIANO
I will not leave thee if thou'lt dwell with me
For wealth of Indies, be my loved boy,
Come in with me, thus Ile begin to do
Some recompence for dead Antonio.

[Exeunt.

SCENE II

Another Room in the Same

[Enter **BERINTHIA**.

BERINTHIA
So I will dare my fortune to be cruell,
And like a mountanous peece of earth that suckes
The balls of hot Artillery, I will stand
And weary all the gunshot; oh my soule
Thou hast beene too long icy Alpes of snow;
Have buried my whole nature, it shall now
Turne Element of fire, and fill the ayre
With bearded Comets, threatning death and horrour

For my wrong'd innocence, contemn'd, disgraced,
Nay murther'd, for with Antonio
My breath expired, and I but borrow this
To court revenge for justice, if there be
Those furies which doe waite on desperate men,
As some have thought, and guide their hands to mischiefe.
Come from the wombe of night, assist a maide
Ambitious to be made a monster like you;
I will not dread your shapes, I am dispos'd
To be at friendship with you, and want nought
But your blacke aide to seale it.

[Enter **COUNT de MONTE NIGRO** and **ANSILVA**.

COUNT de MONTE NIGRO
First ile locke up thy—

[Gives her gold,

Tongue, and tell thee my honorable meaning, so,
To tell you the truth, it is a love-powder, J had it of the
Brave Doctor, which I would have thee to suger
The Ladies cup withall, for my sake wo't do't:
And if I marry her shat find me a noble
Master, and thou shalt be my chiefe Gentlewoman
In Ordinary; keepe thy body loose, and thou shalt
Want no gowne I warrant thee; wo't do't.

ANSILVA
My Lord, I thinke my Lady is much taken with your
worth already, so that this will be superfluous,

COUNT de MONTE NIGRO
I Nay think she has cause enough, but I have a great
Mind to make an end on't, to tell you true, there are
Halfe a dozen about mee, but I had rather she should have
Me than an other; and my blood is growne so boysterous
For my body, thats another thing; so that if thou wilt
Doe it Ansilva, thou wilt doe thy Lady good service,
And live in the favour of Count de Monte Nigro;
I will make thy children kinne to me, if thou wilt do 't.

ANSILVA
I am your honours handmaid, but—

COUNT de MONTE NIGRO
Heres a Diamond, prethee weare it, be not modest.

ANSILVA
'Tis done my Lord, urge it no further.

COUNT de MONTE NIGRO
But be secret too for my honors sake, we great men
Doe not love to have our actions laid open to the
Broad face of the world, Ile get thee with child,
And marry thee to a Knight, my brave Ansilva, take
The first opportunity.

ANSILVA
Jf there be any vertue in the powder, prepare to
Meete your wishes my noble Lord.

COUNT de MONTE NIGRO
Thy Count de monte nigro expect to be a Lady.

[Exit.

BERINTHIA [Coming forward]
Ansilva!

ANSILVA
Madam.

BERINTHIA
Nay you neede not hide it, I heard the conference,
And know the vertue of the powder, let me see it
Or ile discover all.

[She gives the poder to **BERINTHIA**, who changes the packet.

ANSILVA
I am undone.

BERINTHIA
No, here take it againe, ile not prevent
My sisters happinesse and the Counts desire,
I am no Tell-tale good Ansilva giv't her,
And heavens succeede the operation,
I begge on my knee; feare not Ansilva,
I am all silence.

[Exit.

ANSILVA
Indeede Madam, then shee shall have it presently.

[Exit.

Another Room in the Same.

[Enter **SEBASTIANO, CASTABELLA.**

CASTABELLA
Sir, if the opportunity I use
To comfort you be held a fault, and that
I keepe not distance of a servant, lay it
Upon my love; indeede if it be an errour
It springs out of my duty.

SEBESTIANO
Prethee boy be patient;
The more I strive to throw off the remembrance
Of dead Antonio, love still rubbes the wounds
To make them bleede afresh.

CASTABELLA
Alas they are past,
Binde up your owne for honours sake,
And shew love to your selfe, pray do not lose your reason,
To make your griefe so fruitlesse; I have procur'd
Some musicke sir to quiet those sad thoughts,
That makes such warre within you.

[Music within.

SEBESTIANO
Alas good boy, it will but adde more weights
Of dulnesse on me, I am stung with worse
Than the Tarantula, to be cur'd with musicke
'T has the exactest unity, but it cannot,
Accord my thoughts.

CASTABELLA
Sir this your couch
Seemes to invite so small repose;
Oh I beseech you taste it, ile begge
A little leave to sing;

[She sings.

[**SEBASTIANO** throws himself on the couch, and falls asleep.

[Enter **BERINTHIA**.

Sweete sleepe charme his sad sences, and gentle
Thoughts let fall your flowing numbers, here round
About hover caelestiall Angels with your wings
That none offend his quiet, sleepe begins
To cast his nets o're me too, ile obey,
And dreame on him, that dreames not what I am.

[Sleeps.

BERINTHIA [Coming forward]
Nature doth wrestle with me, but revenge
Doth arme my love against it, justice is
Above all tie of blood Sebastiano
Thou art the first shalt tell Antonioes ghost
How much I lov'd him.

[She stabbes him upon his couch]

[**CASTABELLA** awakes in a fright, and rushes out.

SEBESTIANO
Oh stay thy hand Berinthia! Oh,
Th'ast done't, I wish thee heavens forgivenesse, I cannot
Tarry to heare thy reasons, at many doores,
My life runnes out, and yet Berinthia
Doth in her name give me more wounds then these,
Antonio, oh Antonio, we shall now
Be friendes againe.

[Dies.

BERINTHIA
Hees dead, and yet I live, but not to fall
Lesse then a conftellation, more flames must
Make up the fire that Berinthia
And her revenge, must bathe in.

[Enter **CATALINA** poysoned, pulling **ANSILVIA** by the haire.

CASTABELLA
Sebastiano! Sister!

ANSILVA

Murder!

CATALINA
Theres wild-fire in my bowells, sure I am poysoned;
Oh Berinthia.

BERINTHIA
Ha! ha!

CATALINA
Helpe me to teare Ansilva, I am poysoned by
The Count and this fury.

BERINTHIA
Ha! Ha!

CATALINA
Doe you laugh hell-cat?

BERINTHIA
Yes queene of hell to see thee
Sinke in the glory of thy hope for blisse:
But art sure th' art poysoned, Ha!

ANSILVA
Nay I have my part on't, I did but sip, and my belly
Swells too; call you this love-powder, Count Monte
Nigro hath poysoned us both.

BERINTHIA
Y'are a paire of witches, and because
Ile keepe your potion working, know y'are both
Poyson'd by me, by me Berinthia,
Being thus tormented with my wrongs,
I arm'd my selfe with all provision
For my revenge, and had in readinesse
That faithfull poyson which ith' opportunity
I put upon Ansilva for the exchange
Of the amorous powder; oh fooles, my soule
Ravish thy selfe with laughter, politsion
My eldest devil sister! does the heate
Offend your stomacke, troth charity, a little charitie
Th'onely Antidote, thats cold enough:
Looke heres Sebastiano;
Now horrour strike thy soule, to whose fearelesse heart
I sent this punyard, for Antonioes death;
And if that peece of thy damnation
Ansilva had not don't, I meant to have writ

Revenge with the same point upon thy breast;
But I doe surfeit in this brave prevention:
Sleepe, sleepe Antonioes ashes, and now ope
Thou marbell chest to take Berinthia
To mingle with his dust.
Wounds her selfe.

CATALINA
I have not so much heart as to curse, must I die?

[Enter **GASPAR de VILAREZO**, **CASTABELLA**, **COUNT de MOUNTE NIGRO**.

CASTABELLA
Here my Lord, alas hees dead, my Sebastiano

GASPAR DE VILAREZO
Catalina!

CATALINA
I am poyson'd.

GASPAR DE VILAREZO
Ha! Defend good heaven, by whom?

ANSILVA
I am poysoned too.

GASPAR DE VILAREZO
Racke not my soule amazement! T'is a dreame sure.

ANSILVA
Your Love-powder hath poysoned us both.

COUNT de MONTE NIGRO
What will become of me now, I would I were hang'd
To be out of my paine, by this flesh, as I am a Count.
I bought it of the Doctor for good love-powder;
But Madam I hope you are not poysoned in earnest.

CATALINA
The devil on your foolship! oh I must walke
The darke foggy way that spits fire and brimstone,
No physicke to restore me? send for Sharkino, a cooler
A cooler, there a Smiths forge in my belly, and the
Devill blowes the Bellowes, Snow-water, Berinthia
Has poysoned me, sinke by mine owne engine;
I must hence, hence, farewell, will you let me die so?

Confusion, torment, death, hell.

MOUNTE NIGRO
I am glad with all my heart that Berinthia has
Poysoned her, yet—

BERINTHIA
Oh it becomes thee bravely, heare me sir [To **VILAREZO**].
Antonioes death and my dishonours now
Have just revenge; I stabb'd Sebastiano, poysoned my sister,
Oh but they made too soone a fury of me,
And split the patience, from whose dreadfull breach
Came these consuming fires, your passions fruitless;
My soule is reeling forth I know not whether;
Oh father my heart weepes teares, for you I dye, oh see
A maides revenge with her owne Tragedy.

CATALINA
Ansilva, oh thou dull wretch, hell on thy cursed
Weakenesse, thou gavest me
The poyson, but I licke earth, hold, a gentleman
Vsher to support me, oh I am gone, the poyson
Now hath torne my heart in peeces.

[Dies.

GASPAR DE VILAREZO
I am Planet strucke, a direfull Tragedy, and have
I no part in't: how doe you like it, Ha! wast not
Done toth' life? they are my owne children; this was
My eldest girle, this Berinthia the Tragedian,
Whose love by me resisted, was mother of all this
Horror; and theres my boy too, that slew Antonio
Valiantly, and fell under his sisters rage, what
Art thou boy?

CASTABELLA
Ile tell you now I am no boy,
But haplesse Castabella, sister to
The slaine Antonio, I had hop'd to have
Some recompence by Sebastianoes love,
For whose sake in disguise I thus adventur'd
To purchase it, but death hath ravisht us,
And here I bury all my joyes on earth.

COUNT de MONTE NIGRO
Sweet lady, heres Count de Monte Nigro alive
To be your servant.

CASTABELLA
Hence dull greatnesse.

GASPAR DE VILAREZO
Were you a friend of Sebastiano then?

CASTABELLA
Ile give you testimony.

GASPAR DE VILAREZO
No, I beleeve you, but thou canst not be my daughter;
Tis false, he lies that sayes Berinthia
Was author of their deathes, 'twas Villarezo,
A fathers wretched curiosity, dead, dead, dead!

CASTABELLA
And I will leave the world too, for I meane
To spend the poore remainder of my dayes
In some Religious house, married to heaven,
And holy prayers for Sebastianoes soule,
And my lost brother.

GASPAR DE VILAREZO
Will you so?

CASTABELLA
I pray let Castabella have the honour
To enshrine his bones, and when my breath expires,
For sorrow promiseth I shall not live
To see more Sunnes, let me be buried by him
As neere as may be possible, that in death
Our dust may meete, oh my Sebastiano,
Thy wounds are mine.

GASPAR DE VILAREZO
Come I am arm'd, take up their bodies, Castabella you
Are not chiefe mourner here, he was my sonne,
Remember that, Berinthia first, she was the
Youngest, put her ith' pithole first, then Catalina;
Strow, strow flowers enough upon em, for they
Were maides; now Sebastiano, take him
Up gently, he was all the sonnes I had; now
March, come you and I are twinnes in this dayes
Vnhappinesse, wee'le match together, follow close
Wee'le overtake em, softly, and as we go,
Wee'le dare our fortune for another woe.

[*Exeunt* **GASPAR de VILAREZO**, **CASTABELLA** and **COUNT de MONTE NIGRO**, **ATTENDANTS** bearing the bodies before them.

FINIS.

JAMES SHIRLEY – A CONCISE BIBLIOGRAPHY

The following includes years of first publication, and of performance if known, together with dates of licensing by the Master of the Revels if available.

TRAGEDIES
The Maid's Revenge (licensed 9th February 1626; printed, 1639)
The Traitor (licensed 4th May 1631; printed, 1635)
Love's Cruelty (licensed 14th November 1631; printed, 1640)
The Politician (acted, 1639; printed, 1655)
The Cardinal (licensed 25th May 1641; printed, 1652).

TRAGI-COMEDIES
The Grateful Servant (licensed 3rd November 1629 as The Faithful Servant; printed 1630)
The Young Admiral (licensed 3rd July 1633; printed 1637)
The Coronation (licensed 6th February 1635, as Shirley's, but printed in 1640 as a work of John Fletcher)
The Duke's Mistress (licensed 18th January 1636; printed 1638)
The Gentleman of Venice (licensed 30th October 1639; printed 1655)
The Doubtful Heir (printed 1652), licensed as Rosania, or Love's Victory in 1640
The Imposture (licensed 10th November 1640; printed 1652)
The Court Secret (printed 1653).

COMEDIES
Love Tricks, or the School of Complement (licensed 10th February 1625; printed under its subtitle, 1631)
The Wedding (ca. 1626; printed 1629)
The Brothers (licensed 4th November 1626; printed 1652)
The Witty Fair One (licensed 3rd October 1628; printed 1633)
The Humorous Courtier (licensed 17th May 1631; printed 1640).
The Changes, or Love in a Maze (licensed 10th January 1632; printed 1639)
Hyde Park (licensed 20th April 1632; printed 1637)
The Ball (licensed 16th November 1632; printed 1639)
The Bird in a Cage, or The Beauties (licensed 21st January 1633; printed 1633)
The Gamester (licensed 11th November 1633; printed 1637)
The Example (licensed 24th June 1634; printed 1637)
The Opportunity (licensed 29th November 1634; printed 1640)
The Lady of Pleasure (licensed 15th October 1635; printed 1637)
The Royal Master (acted and printed 1638)
The Constant Maid, or Love Will Find Out the Way (printed 1640)
The Sisters (licensed 26th April 1642; printed 1653).
Honoria and Mammon (printed 1659)